THE HUMAN FACTOR
IN COMMUNITY
WORK

THE HUMAN FACTOR
IN COMMUNITY
WORK

T. R. BATTEN

with the collaboration of
MADGE BATTEN

LONDON
OXFORD UNIVERSITY PRESS
1965

Oxford University Press, Amen House, London E.C.4

GLASGOW NEW YORK TORONTO MELBOURNE WELLINGTON
BOMBAY CALCUTTA MADRAS KARACHI LAHORE DACCA
CAPE TOWN SALISBURY NAIROBI IBADAN ACCRA
KUALA LUMPUR HONG KONG

© *Oxford University Press 1965*

Printed in Great Britain by
The Camelot Press Ltd., London and Southampton

Contents

PREFACE   vii

I   INTRODUCTION   I

II   MEETING REQUESTS FOR HELP   6

    1. The Unused Library   7
    2. Local Government   10
    3. The Brick Factory   14
    4. The Recreation Ground   18
    Conclusions   22
    Implications for the Worker   22

III   SUGGESTING COMMUNITY PROJECTS   25

    5. Preventing Floods   25
    6. Eradicating Mosquitoes   28
    7. Making-up the Road   32
    8. The Want that Wasn't Felt   36
    Conclusions   38
    Implications for the Worker   39

IV   INTRODUCING IMPROVEMENTS   42

    9. Helping the Farmers   42
    10. The Bee Expert   46
    11. The Cassava Graters   49
    12. Conserving the Soil   52
    13. Turning Nomads into Farmers   55
    14. The Chartered Bus   58
    15. Improving Homesteads   62
    Conclusions   66
    Implications for the Worker   69

V   ESTABLISHING GROUPS   72

    16. The Parent–Teacher Association   72
    17. The Village Co-operative   77

18. The Tamarind Tree Group   80
19. The Grocery Store   85
    Conclusions   88
    Implications for the Worker   90

VI WORKING WITH GROUPS   92
20. The Community Project that Wasn't   92
21. He Meant Well   99
22. The Nursery School   104
    Conclusions   108

VII WORKING WITH LEADERS   110
23. The Sheikh and the Schoolmaster   110
24. The Chief of Ikam   113
25. The New Village Hall   117
26. The Would-be Benefactors   120
    Conclusions   123

VIII DEALING WITH FACTION   126
27. The Rival Leaders   126
28. The Majority Vote   130
29. The District Councillor   134
30. Negri Village   140
31. Politics and People   145
    Conclusions   149

IX ASKING FOR HELP   154
32. The Dissatisfied Volunteers   154
33. The Practice School   159
34. The Disappointed Villagers   163
35. The Homemakers' Class   167
36. The Horse Disease   170
37. The 3-F Campaign   173
    Conclusions   177

X SUMMARY OF CONCLUSIONS   181

Preface

By 'community work' in this book we mean any and every organized attempt to encourage, educate, influence or help people to become actively involved in meeting some of their own needs. From this standpoint all organizations engaged in community development, social development, adult education, agricultural extension, health extension, and co-operative education, as well as women's organizations and youth organizations, are promoting some form of community work. The content of their programmes may be very different, but they are all working with *people* and have basically similar problems in achieving their purposes with them.

This book is primarily intended for the field workers, supervisors and local administrators of such organizations. It contains thirty-seven cases drawn from almost as many countries, both 'developing' and 'developed', and each of these cases presents a problem.

Each case is followed by a commentary which analyses the problem and discusses its implications for the worker. This commentary reflects the ideas contributed in discussion by an international group of experienced field officers and administrators who decided to study the case because they felt that the problem it presented was typical of a kind of problem they frequently encountered in their own countries, and which often defeated them as it had defeated the worker in the actual case. The main purpose of the commentaries, however, is not so much to provide specific 'solutions' as to clarify *why* the worker failed, and then to suggest *how*, by modifying his approach, he might have significantly increased his chances of success.

The cases are grouped into chapters on the basis of the kind of problem they present, and each chapter ends with a statement of general conclusions for the guidance of workers faced with similar problems.

Some readers may feel that too much space in the commentaries is given to discussion of details of behaviour and approach, but we do not share this view. It is just what the worker does, and with what result, in each and every situation in which he works face-to-face with the members of each small local committee or group that affects the success or failure of even the biggest national programme: and in this book we are concerned with the *details* that make for success.

Although this book is primarily intended for those who work in or very close to the field, we also hope that senior administrators, and more especially those who have not had first-hand experience of working in the field themselves, will be helped to understand more clearly the true nature of some of the many difficulties with which their workers have to try to deal. Although the commentaries are firmly focused on the implications of the cases for the *worker*, it will be obvious to the reader that almost every case also has implications for the senior officials who control and direct his work. In fact, all too often they are at least partly responsible for his failures, either by setting him unrealistic targets or by denying him enough time or freedom of action to enable him to achieve them.

Lastly, many trainers have told us that they have difficulty in obtaining suitable case material for use on their training courses. This book, we hope, will help to meet their need.

T. R. Batten
Madge Batten

University of London
   Institute of Education
   1965

CHAPTER ONE

Introduction

NOWADAYS in every country there are very many agencies, both government and voluntary, which are in some way concerned with development—that is, with promoting change for the better. Some forms of development can be planned and implemented without the common people being consulted or involved. Other forms of development, however, can only take place to the extent that ordinary people agree with them, want them, and are willing to implement them themselves. Thus agencies which aim at promoting changes in peasant agriculture, in diet, in health practices, or in child care in the home, equally with those which aim at influencing people's attitudes and behaviour towards each other, must primarily depend on the skill of their workers in educating, influencing, and stimulating people to act.

What criteria can we use to measure success in this kind of work? Is it enough, for instance, that the worker should achieve his immediate purpose, whether this is to get the people to plant a new kind of seed; use fertilizer on their farms; build latrines; form a co-operative; join a literacy class; or undertake the building of a road, a dam, a fishpond, a school, a village hall, or whatever other self-help project they may decide on? In fact, this is not enough, for the worker will still have failed if the people, having given the new seeds or the fertilizer a trial, give up using it because they become dissatisfied with the results they get; or having built latrines do not use them; or having learnt to read become illiterate again; or having built the road soon cannot use it because they fail to maintain it in good repair. For development to take place—for the worker really to succeed —the changes he promotes must have some lasting good effect.

But perhaps even this criterion is inadequate, for many

development agencies now aim to make the people with whom they work enterprising and self-reliant, more ready to face up to the need for further change, and more willing to work together for the good of their community. If the worker plans and organizes and helps too much, the result may be to make people more rather than less dependent on outside stimulus and help. Again, if the effect of what he does, however unintended, is to increase bad feeling in the community, the people will become less willing to work together on future projects for the common good.

The more we think of development as a continuing process, each stage of which has some effect—good or bad—on the attitude of people to the succeeding stage, the more concerned we shall be about the effect of each stage of development on the attitudes and relationships of the people.

We have already noted that the worker may have both a short-term purpose (to get the people to take some specific action), and also a long-term purpose (to make the people more self-reliant and willing to work together), and that he may sometimes achieve the first at the expense of the second to the prejudice of future work. But if he also fails to achieve even his short-term purpose this, too, may have adverse results. Thus every time a worker sponsors an idea which the people reject, so he decreases their confidence in himself as a person who really is able to help them. This is true even when he proposes a change that the people reject outright, for in rejecting the change, in effect they are also rejecting him: and if they think him wrong on this occasion they will be all the more ready to think him wrong on others. This adverse effect will be still worse if he succeeds in getting them to accept a change which turns out badly. The people will then feel that the worker has misled them, and they will be much less willing to co-operate when he returns to suggest a change of any other kind. Nor is this adverse effect limited only to the community in which the failure occurred. People talk, and once mistrust is sown in one community it can quickly spread to others.

Since failures threaten the prospects of success in future work, as well as wasting current effort, it is highly desirable to avoid them. And while it would be quite unrealistic for any agency or worker to expect to be able to avoid failures altogether, there would certainly be fewer if only more thought and care were taken in order to avoid them. No one wants failure, and no one will deliberately commit himself to a project which he knows will fail. Rather he will abandon it in favour of some other project with which he thinks he will succeed. Always he plans and works in the hope and expectation of success, and if he fails he fails because of some misjudgement or mistake that he has made. Either his choice, or his planning, or his skill will have been at fault: and the administrator or field worker can best equip himself to avoid the same faults in future by diagnosing the cause of his failures in order to identify what these faults are, and by reflecting upon what, in the light of this study, he could more usefully have done. To the extent that he can make these diagnoses correctly, and draw out the right conclusions from them, he is then able to profit from his experience to the maximum extent. However, to train himself to do this effectively he may need help both in the practice of diagnosis and in drawing conclusions from it. It is to provide some such help that we present the cases we have selected for inclusion in this book.

These cases are all real in the sense that the events they describe actually happened. Only the names of people and places have been changed. They have been contributed by administrators and workers from many countries, and have been selected from a much larger number of cases as those which best illustrate the most common causes of failure. The cases are grouped into chapters, and each chapter deals with a problem of a different kind. Each problem is therefore investigated in the context of several of the contributed cases.

The 'worker' in any particular case may variously be a district commissioner, a community development officer, a social welfare worker, an organizer of adult literacy classes, a schoolmaster, a co-operative officer, a health worker, or an agricultural extension officer. The specific purposes which these different kinds of worker pursue are not in themselves significant for the purpose of the study, since each case illustrates some problem of working with people which any of these workers may commonly meet in the work he has to do. Thus each can learn by studying the work experience of the others. Nor do we need to take the differences in cultural setting very seriously into account, for the basic factors which give rise to these problems are the same everywhere, however much their cultural expression may vary. Thus for example it is generally true, whatever the culture, that people will not willingly accept an innovation, or persist with it having once accepted it, unless they are convinced that it will bring some real advantage to themselves; that they will tend to resent criticism of their existing way of life by an outsider, however well-intentioned such an outsider may be; that they will not willingly co-operate with any person or group they feel they have good reason to mistrust; and that they will tend to oppose any change that seems likely, in their opinion, to lessen their own status or increase the status of their rivals. The main value to be derived from a study of the cases lies in the insights this can provide into the implications that factors such as these may have for administrators and workers in *any* culture.

Each case gives information about how a worker tried to help a group of people. It describes his purpose, what he did in order to achieve it, and the result. In each case this result, in the opinion of the worker, was that he had failed. Each case therefore presents the reader with a challenge to think out why the worker failed and what alternative approach, had he adopted it, might have given him a better chance of success.

Those readers who attempt to think out these conclusions for themselves are those who will profit most from their study of this book. To such readers we venture to make the following suggestions:

A. *Each case*

1. First read the case, but leave the commentary unread.
2. Assess it for relevance and typicality. (Each case is a local and specific example of a general problem, and to get the most

value from studying a case, it is first necessary to recognize it as an example of such a problem. For instance, Case 1 takes place in an urban situation and the project the people undertook was the provision of a library, but its real value is that it is a specific example of the common problem *that people will often undertake a project for which they have no real use when they have completed it.*)

3. Assess the situation as it was at the beginning of the case in terms of the people's readiness to consider change; their attitude to the worker; and their attitudes to each other (e.g. how co-operative or uncooperative they originally were).

4. Assess the situation at the end of the case, noting in what respects it has improved or deteriorated (e.g. are the people satisfied with their achievement? are they as a result more, or less, willing to contemplate further change? have they now greater, or less, confidence in the worker? are they now more, or less, willing to co-operate with one another for common purposes?).

5. In the light of the above assessments, define the exact nature of the worker's achievement and assess the extent of his failure.

6. Diagnose the reasons for his failure by listing the factors he neglected to take into account and whatever mistakes he may seem to have made in his choice of approach.

7. In the light of this diagnosis think out specifically just how he might have increased his chances of success.

8. Read the commentary and compare its conclusions with one's own.

B. *Each chapter*

1. List one's own general conclusions based on one's study of the cases included in the chapter.

2. Compare with the conclusions stated at the end of that chapter.

CHAPTER TWO

Meeting Requests for Help

IN each of the cases presented in this book, we see a worker trying to encourage and help the members of some local community or community group to undertake a project or accept an innovation which he or his agency thinks will be of some real benefit to them. In each case he fails, and this might seem to reinforce the idea, already quite commonly held, that most people dislike change and will resist it if they can. This idea, however, ignores the fact that people in every culture have modified their way of life in the past and are still doing so today. The truth seems to be that most people will readily accept change, but only when certain conditions are met. These are, first, that they should want the change for the benefit they expect to result; secondly, that they should know, or think they know, both what they need to do and also how to do it; thirdly, that they should have, or think they have, whatever resources they need in order to do what is needed to put the change into effect; and fourthly, that where joint action is required, as in a group or community project, they should be willing to work together for the common good.

Whenever all these conditions are present, people will usually act without waiting for any external help or advice: and if they were always present in every community in relation to each and every conceivable need, development agencies and their workers would not be needed. But very often one or more of these conditions is lacking, and it is then the job of the worker to do whatever is necessary to ensure that they are met.

This job is sometimes very easy and sometimes very hard. It is hardest, other things being equal, when the worker has to try to get people to implement changes that he or his agency thinks are needed, but which the people themselves are not yet aware of needing. It is easiest when the people already know what they want to do, so that only encouragement, advice, and a little help are needed. It is easiest of all, one might think, when, as in all the cases included in the chapter, the people come to the worker to state their want and seek his help. Yet even then some foresight and skill are needed, as a study of the following cases will show.

1. THE UNUSED LIBRARY

The people of a poor urban neighbourhood seek the worker's help in connexion with a project they have already decided on.

THE CASE

I am a social development officer. I work in a large seaside town and most of my responsibilities are with the poorer people who live near the docks. There are several distinct neighbourhoods in this area. Each neighbourhood has its own unofficially elected committee, and naturally I make use of these committees in connexion with my work.

For some time before the events I am about to describe took place I had been trying to get these committees interested in doing something to improve the amenities of their neighbourhoods, but without much success. Therefore I was very pleased when the members of one of the committees invited me to a meeting to discuss a project which they had decided on for themselves. This was the building of a small library and reading room for the people of the neighbourhood to use. They told me when I met them that everyone was strongly in favour of it and that they had already chosen a site. This was on a piece of waste-land that belonged to the town council, and they hoped that I would help them by getting the council to agree to let them have it. As far as the building was concerned, they said the people were willing to give their labour free and also to raise money to pay for at least some of the materials and equipment needed. As for the cost of maintaining the library when it had been built, it had been agreed that users of the library would pay a small monthly subscription so that there would always be funds available for that.

This all seemed sound enough to me, so we then got down to discussing plans and costs. In the end we concluded that £300 would be needed for building materials and a further £200 for equipment and books. Of this total of £500 the committee members said they could raise half if the town council would provide the remaining half.

In due course I put the project to the town council which received it very favourably. The council agreed to provide the site and £250 on condition that the people were able to raise their share of the money and build the library themselves. All went well. The money was raised, the library built and stocked with books, and someone was found who agreed to look after the library for a small monthly wage. Then there was a grand opening ceremony at which the mayor declared the library open. At this ceremony I received many compliments.

Then, a few weeks later, the chairman and secretary of the committee came to see me because they were already very worried about the future of the library. The people liked it all right. In fact, they were so proud of it that they brought all their friends and relatives to see it. The trouble was that hardly any of them had enrolled as library members because, so they said, they really had very little time for reading. This meant that so few people were paying subscriptions that the committee could not pay the librarian his wages, and they were afraid, therefore, that the library might have to be closed.

In the end, that is just what did happen. I did my best and so did the committee members, but most of the people still refused to join and the town council rejected my application for further help. Thus within a few months of the opening ceremony, the library was closed and all the people's effort and money wasted. If they had no real use for a library, then why did they go to so much trouble to get one?

DISCUSSION OF THE CASE

Diagnosis

At first the members of the group which discussed this case had some difficulty in pinpointing just where the social development officer had gone wrong. Superficially, he seemed to have done all the right things unless, as some members suggested, he had relied too much on what the members of the local committee had told him. They thought that the idea of the library project probably originated in the committee, and that if the committee were not truly representative of the common people, this would account for the choice of a project the people did not really want. They thought that he should have got the

committee to call a public meeting of the people of the neighbourhood so that he could have discussed the project with them and
tested their reactions to it. If he had done this, they thought, he
might well have discovered that most of the people were much
less keen on having a library than the committee members
would have had him believe.

This suggestion was argued at some length, but it was then
agreed that while it was always desirable for a worker to check
the representativeness of the committee or group with which he
works, the facts in this case in no way supported the idea that
this particular committee was unrepresentative. After all, the
neighbourhood was a poor one, but in spite of this the committee had been able to raise £250 in cash for the project. It
could hardly have collected so large a sum if the people had not
wanted a library; nor could it have got them to give their labour
free. Indeed, everything suggested that the people wanted a
library in their neighbourhood even if they did not want to use
it as a source of reading for themselves.

This faced the group with the problem of trying to understand why people should want a library badly enough to raise
money for it and work for it if they had no apparent use for it.
This led to a long discussion at the end of which all members
of the group were agreed that the most likely reason was that
although most individuals in the neighbourhood had little use
for reading—after all they were mostly manual workers and
probably ill-educated—as a neighbourhood they wanted the
library primarily for the status they felt it would give them in
the eyes of the people of the other neighbourhoods in the dock
area. This, the group felt, was the only explanation that would
meet all the facts: the sacrifices the people were willing to make
to get the library; their pride in showing it to people from other
neighbourhoods; and their reluctance, as individuals, to use it
for reading.

At this point in the discussion several of the group's members
contributed from their experience supporting examples to illustrate the great influence that status considerations may have in
distorting the choice of a project by an under-privileged group.

B

Implications

The members of the group then discussed the implications of their diagnosis for the worker. Had he suspected that status reasons might have influenced the people's choice of project, they thought, he would have tried to find out just how many people really wanted to join the library as reading members: and he would not have committed himself to sponsor the project with the town council until he had satisfied himself that enough people would enrol as reading members to enable the maintenance costs to be met.

While all members of the group agreed on this point, they were less clear about how he could have got the information he needed. It would be difficult for him to contact each family head individually, and they thought that a show of hands at a public meeting might well be misleading. In the end they felt that the best approach to solving this problem was for him to get the committee's members to collect the necessary information for him. But how could he be sure that the information they provided was true? Mainly, the group thought, by helping the committee's members to see how dependent in fact they were, if they wished to ensure the success of the project, on knowing that enough people felt seriously committed to subscribe, and go on subscribing, as reading members. Once the committee's members clearly realized that to go ahead with the project without sure information on this point would be to invite failure, they themselves would be keen to get it: and if they were not satisfied with it when they had got it, they would probably decide to abandon the library project in favour of ome other project which had a better chance of success.

2. LOCAL GOVERNMENT

The people come to their administrative officer with their problem and he tells them what he thinks they ought to do.

THE CASE

In my country there are local government councils in some areas but not in others. Where local government councils have been set up they have the power to raise taxes to pay for the local services they provide. It is government policy to encourage people in the non-local government areas to opt for the setting up of local government councils, but they are often unwilling to do this as they do not want to pay taxes to a local government in addition to the tax they already pay to the central government.

I am an administrative officer in charge of a district. One day a deputation of farmers of one area came to my office to complain that they had no good water-supply for drinking purposes and no good drains to carry excess rainwater away from their farms. Since the provision of pure water and improved drainage are among the recognized functions of local government councils, I thought this gave me a good chance of getting the people of this area to agree to set up a local government council. Therefore I told them that this was what I thought they ought to do, and suggested that they should call a meeting at which I would explain the procedure.

In due course I went to the meeting and talked to them about the advantages of local government, telling them that this was the way they could solve their problems of water-supply and drainage. I explained that they would have to pay a local government tax, but pointed out some of the tax money would be used to provide them with the local services they now wanted.

None of the people had ever before paid taxes to a local government and they did not like the idea at all. They paid taxes to the central government, they said, and they thought it was up to the central government to help them now. They said that they were poor men and that local government was a luxury they could not afford.

I talked with them for a long time in the hope that they would change their minds, but without any effect. They are still without a local government and their water-supply and drains are still un-improved. And so I suppose I failed, but do you think you could have done better?

Diagnosis   DISCUSSION OF THE CASE

The members of the group which discussed this case thought that they would probably have acted as the district officer had done had they been in his situation, but when they had con-sidered the case for a bit they became critical of what he had done on several counts. They noticed, for instance, that he seemed much more interested in pushing his government's policy than in helping the people to think out a solution for themselves. Thus he offered only the one ready-made solution which fitted in best with his own purposes—to get the people of the area to accept local government—but which *to the people* seemed to fit in very badly with theirs. He gave them no opportunity to explore any alternative, and he took no action to get their water-supply and drainage problems investigated by any officer of a government technical department. The total effect on the people, the group thought, must have been to make them feel that their district officer was not in the least interested in trying to help them solve their problems, but only in taking advantage of their present difficulties to get them to conform to what he wanted them to do: and the more they felt like this about the district officer, the more opposed they would be to accepting his suggestion.

Implications

The group felt that he could have done more to help the people, avoid arousing their resentment, and incidentally increase his chances of getting them to consider local government as *one* possible solution, if he had shown much greater interest in helping the people to solve their problems as they saw them. This would have meant, they thought:

A. *When he met the deputation*

1. listening carefully and patiently to all they had to say;
2. asking questions to get more detailed information about specific points;
3. stating quite clearly what kind of help they might expect the central government to give, e.g. what technical advice and what material help; and also, equally clearly, what the people would have to be prepared to do for themselves, e.g. provide labour, raise money, collect materials;
4. suggesting that he (or the people) should ask officers of the appropriate technical departments to visit the area to check up on exactly what needed to be done;
5. offering to attend a meeting of the people in the area to discuss possible ways of tackling their two problems when more of the detailed facts were known.

B. *When he met the people of the area*

1. stating quite clearly what government would and would not do to help;

2. helping the people to assess just how much effort they themselves would have to make;

3. stimulating the people to think out quite concretely how they felt they would best be able to do their share (by forming a co-operative? by organizing a project under the self-help scheme? by opting for local government? by . . .?);

4. helping the people to consider all the pros and cons of each alternative with a view to choosing that which suited them best.

The group felt that this approach would have been better in several ways. By stating clearly both what he could and could not do to help, the district officer would have got his discussions with the people on to a sound and realistic basis from the start. By helping them to think clearly about what they themselves would need to do, by offering to help them get the technical advice they needed, and by encouraging them to explore any and every possible solution with a view to finding the one that suited them best, he would have been demonstrably working in the people's interest instead of doing what he actually did, which was to argue against them in his own. If he had done all this, there would indeed still have been no certainty that the people would have chosen local government as their solution; but at any rate they would then have been able to consider it as one alternative without being prejudiced against it by the district officer's attempt to force it on them. And this, if local government really was the best solution, would have increased its chances of adoption. There would have been other advantages too. By helping and encouraging the people to think and decide for themselves, the district officer would have been helping them better to understand at least some of their responsibilities as citizens. In addition, by clearly and consistently demonstrating his real desire to help them, he would have avoided arousing their resentment and made it more likely that they would again seek his help in the future.

3. THE BRICK FACTORY

A small group of village people tell the worker what they want to do and ask for help. They find the outcome disappointing and lose confidence in the worker as a result.

THE CASE

I am a community worker in a country which suffered a good deal during the last war. One day last year I was visited by a group of six men all of whom came from the same village. They explained that they were anxious to restart what had been a flourishing little brick-making factory before it had been destroyed during the last war, and which had not been restarted since because no one had had enough money to rebuild it. They said, however, that they had now formed a co-operative society into which they were putting their savings, and they were also hoping to get a government grant towards the cost of the building and the necessary machinery. There were many unemployed men in the village and everyone wanted the factory for the employment it would give. Could I do anything to help?

I said that I would be very willing to help them prepare their application for a government grant, and that I could probably help them in other ways too. But, I said, were they quite sure that they would be able to make a success of the project in view of all the changes that had taken place since the war? I thought an expert opinion was needed and offered to get an economist to study the situation and report on whether the project was likely to succeed or not.

The men agreed that this might be a good idea. I found a suitable expert and after a short time he made his report. In this report he advised against the project mainly because he thought the men would have great trouble in selling their bricks since they would now have to compete with the products of several big, modern brick-making factories. The men were very disappointed, and so were the people of the village from which they had come. The people were now divided, some arguing that they should go ahead with the project in spite of the expert's adverse report while many others were now afraid to try. This stirred up much bad feeling and in the end the project was abandoned. I was glad it was abandoned, for I didn't think it had much chance of success, but the whole episode has certainly had a bad effect on the villagers' attitude to me. Many of them think that I was not a bit interested in trying to help them, and some of them even think that I caused the project to fail. Was this result inevitable, or could I have avoided it if I had acted differently?

DISCUSSION OF THE CASE

All the members of the group which discussed this case agreed that its outcome—the people's loss of confidence in the good intentions of the worker—was something that workers should always try to avoid, but some members felt that in this case it was unavoidable and that they had therefore nothing to learn by discussing it. Others, however, felt that they could learn something from it and in the end it was accepted for discussion.

The group then decided on two lines of inquiry: the first, to decide on just what the worker did that led people to think that he did not really want to help them; and the second, in the light of this diagnosis to reach conclusions about what the worker should preferably have done.

Diagnosis

After some discussion of the worker's conduct, the members of the group felt that they were beginning to understand much better why people became suspicious and mistrustful. They listed their reasons as follows:

1. Apparently the worker was content to deal exclusively with the six men who came to see him, although many of the village people also felt involved since they all wanted to see the factory re-established for the employment it would bring to the village. In spite of this, the worker appeared to have made no attempt to discuss the project with these people. They therefore had no way of finding out how things were going except from the six men most directly concerned.

2. The worker did not help and encourage even these men to think out their own conclusions for themselves. Instead, he took the lead in suggesting that the project might fail. This was psychologically bad, especially as the men were so anxious that the project should succeed. He could have made this point quite as effectively and more positively if he had stressed the

need for them to find and investigate every possible snag *in order to ensure that the project should succeed.*

3. The worker both suggested the need for an expert opinion and chose the expert himself. This meant that the people would regard the expert as the worker's agent and his opinion as the worker's opinion. This was also psychologically bad especially if, as the worker expected, the report turned out to be disappointing. Preferably the worker should have contented himself with asking questions until the men themselves realized that they could not answer some of the questions without some outside help, and *then* made his suggestion. Also, he should have asked the expert to limit his report to stating facts from which the men could then have drawn their own conclusions. (Incidentally, some members of the group doubted whether the expert was really as competent to pass judgement on this project as the worker thought. His judgement appeared to be based on purely general grounds and without much reference to local circumstances. The people, for instance, might have been able to compete successfully with the larger factories in making bricks for purely local sale, and they might have been willing to work for unusually low wages rather than have no work at all.)

4. Once the expert had reported adversely, the workers seemed to have been content to leave things at that in spite of the people's underlying need for economic help. Members of the group thought that he could have done a good deal to restore confidence in himself if he had gone out to the village to get people interested in finding some alternative project which would have a better chance of success.

Implications

The members of the group felt that there were two parts to this problem: the one, how he should have handled his discussions with the men; and the other, what action, if any, he should have taken in the community from which the men came.

He would have made a more favourable impression on the six men, the group thought, if, after listening carefully to all they had to say and promising to do his best to help them, he had told them quite specifically what conditions they would have to satisfy when they applied for a government grant: e.g. they would have to provide plans and a statement of costs; they would have to show that they had sufficient working capital; and they would have to provide other information to prove that their project was really sound. He could then have suggested that they would need this information for themselves as well, if only to safeguard their savings by avoiding needless risks of failure.

This would have provided him with a reason for asking a whole range of questions about how they proposed to maintain themselves in competition with the existing suppliers of bricks. The group thought that the men would be able to find answers to some of these questions from their local knowledge of their own and neighbouring communities. But they also thought that they might be unable to answer others. It would be at this point, when the men were conscious of needing information they could not get for themselves, that the worker could have suggested enlisting the help of an expert to obtain it for them: and at this point he could have done it without arousing the men's resentment even if the outcome were disappointing. Throughout all the discussion, in fact, the men would then have felt that the worker had been consistently trying to help them without it any way trying to influence their decision about whether they ought to proceed. If he had worked in this way, members of the group felt, he would have increased, not lessened, the respect the men had for him as a person who really was trying to help them.

The group also felt very strongly that the worker should have visited the community from which the men came. Although strictly speaking this was not a community project since the factory would be owned by the co-operative formed by the six men, the whole community wanted it to succeed for the employment it would provide. As a community worker, the group felt he should have been aware of this, and taken the trouble to contact the people and inform them of what he was trying to do. This would have helped him to retain the people's confidence

if and when the project failed. It was even more important that he should visit the community after the failure, partly
in order to show his concern for the people and partly in order
to explore with them other possible means of providing employment. Had he done this, thought the members of the group, the
villagers would have seen him in a quite different light.

4. THE RECREATION GROUND

The people unite to complete a whole series of projects, only
to lose heart when they are on the point of achieving success
with the project that they had originally said they needed most.

THE CASE

There was a village in the district where I was working as a community development officer in which people took no part in any
form of organized social activity. All this changed, however, when a
man from this village, a carpenter, returned from work on a job in
another village. While working in this other village, he had been
very impressed with the variety of its local activities, and with the
many amenities such as street-lighting, a recreation ground, games
equipment, and handicraft classes for the women and girls that the
people had got themselves through their own efforts. He talked
about this on his return to his own village and the people soon
responded enthusiastically. They held a meeting at which they
decided to ask me in to help and advise them.

At their next meeting, at which I was present, they listed many of
their needs. In order of priority these were a recreation ground, a
road, a first-aid centre, and a community centre. At this meeting
the people also elected a committee to organize their work.

They were all so keen that I felt really happy to help them. I was
able to get the local authority to earmark a piece of land for a
recreation ground and was delighted when it promised to have it
put in order at some later date. Otherwise the people did almost
everything for themselves. They not only built themselves a road
but also constructed a temporary shed for use as a community centre
on the land the local authority had set aside for their future recreation ground. This they did although they knew that the shed would
have to be pulled down when the time came to put the recreation
ground in order. They also established a women's group which
learnt how to produce useful articles from local materials; a games

club which competed with clubs from neighbouring villages; and a youth club. All three groups used the community centre which also housed their first-aid kit. The women took special pride in keeping the community centre always clean and tidy.

It was five years before the local authority allocated funds to put the recreation ground in order and at first everyone was delighted. But when they realized that they would have to pull down their community centre, they became most unhappy in spite of the local authority's generous offer to find them a permanent site for a new one. With the loss of their centre the groups stopped meeting, and very soon the people lost interest in all their community activities. Yet up to that time they had all done so well. They had been keen enough to get a recreation ground. Then why did they give up just when they had got it?

DISCUSSION OF THE CASE

Diagnosis

The members of the group which discussed this case decided first to try to understand why the people so suddenly lost interest in the community activities that had flourished so successfully during the previous five years. They felt that the reason for this was the sudden loss of their community centre. Although it was only a shed, the people had built it themselves and seemed to have developed a real affection for it because of all the happy times they had had in it. Thus, when the time came for pulling it down they would probably have felt a bit sad anyway, even if there had been a new centre ready for them to move into, but the real catastrophe was that they had no such alternative centre. It was all very well for the local authority to promise to find them a site for a new permanent centre but meanwhile, and until it was built, the community's groups had nowhere to meet. In these circumstances it was not surprising that the groups soon began to disintegrate.

This seemed a reasonable enough explanation, but some members of the group felt that it left several questions un-answered. If the people valued their centre so much why then did they ever build it on a site where they knew that at some future date they would have to pull it down? Again, if they valued their centre so much, why then did they ever agree to pull it down until they had its replacement ready? After all, they could almost certainly have kept it if they had been prepared to forego having a proper recreation ground. Again, since they did pull it down, why then did they not erect another? After all, their original centre was only a shed and it couldn't have been too hard a job to build another like it.

The members of the group discussed each of these questions in turn. The answer to the first, they felt, was that when the people originally decided to erect their shed they were not at all worried by the thought that they would have to pull it down later on, partly because it was only a shed, and partly because it was only gradually, while they were using it and developing their new activities in it, that they really began to value it and come to depend on it. As to why they did not decide to keep it at the cost of forgoing their recreation ground, the members of the group felt that they still wanted this, and that anyway while they still had their centre they still did not realize just how much they had come to depend on it. In fact, they probably did not fully realize this until *after* they had pulled their centre down. With regard to the third question, members of the group felt that the people might very well have built a new shed to replace the old one if they had known in good time when the old one would have to be destroyed, but the people seem to have been given very little time. The group also felt that the local authority did not help matters by its well-meant offer to provide a permanent site for a new centre at some future time. The people's need was immediate, but the prospect of soon having to build a permanent centre might well have been enough to sway opinion against making the effort to build another temporary shed.

Implications

The root cause of the trouble which overtook this community, the group felt, was that in making their decisions the people consistently failed to think far enough ahead. They built their temporary centre where they knew it would have to be pulled down because they did not realize how much they would come to depend on it. They pulled it down because they wanted the recreation ground and still did not fully realize what it would mean to them to be without a centre. And they did nothing about building a new temporary centre because, by the time they had fully realized their loss, their groups had already disintegrated and everyone had lost heart.

The group did not think that the people should be blamed for this lack of foresight. It was natural, almost inevitable, that they should make mistakes, for they had no previous experience to guide them. The one person who should have been able to guide and help them was the community development officer, but this he quite failed to do at several points and the group listed them as follows:

1. At the outset, when the people were discussing the building of the shed, he should certainly have got them to think out all the pros and cons of where to site it in the hope that they would then choose a site where the shed could remain until they could build a permanent centre.

2. If he had failed at this early stage he should have made sure of knowing well in advance when the local authority would be willing to put the recreation ground in order. He should then have tried to get the people to consider building themselves another shed *before* the old one had to be pulled down. Alternatively, he could have tried to get the local authority to decide on a new site for a permanent centre well before the shed had to be pulled down. The people would then have been in a position to plan (and build) their permanent centre before they lost their old one.

By failing to act in any of these ways, the group felt, the community development worker had neglected one of the most important functions of any community development worker— that of thinking ahead to foresee pitfalls and problems which due to their experience or enthusiasm the people do not see; drawing attention to them; and getting people to think about them before making decisions which they might otherwise later regret.

CONCLUSIONS

Study of the four cases presented in this chapter suggest several conclusions of general significance.

1. *Even when people have already chosen a project, and need only a little encouragement and help to go ahead, the worker still needs to check that the project will meet a real and permanent need.*

(Rivalry between communities and status needs, as we have seen in *The Unused Library*, may sometimes lead people to chose a project, or size of project, for which they have no lasting use. Disillusionment sets in after they have completed the project and then adversely affects their readiness to undertake further projects.)

2. *The worker needs to be able to convince people that he really is keen to help them even while trying to dissuade them from undertaking a project which he thinks is badly chosen and likely to fail.*

(The worker failed to convince people of this in *The Brick Factory*. He would have faced the same problem in Case 1 if he had tried to dissuade them from undertaking the library project.)

3. *The worker must not assume, because the people seek his advice, that all he has to do is to give it, for they won't take it unless they think it good. His real job, therefore is to help them find a solution acceptable to themselves.*

(It was because the worker did not understand this that he failed in *Local Government*.)

4. *The worker should draw the people's attention to factors which they would otherwise overlook, but which they need to take into account when deciding what to do.*

(This conclusion is based on the course of events in *The Recreation Ground*. The people made several bad decisions because they were unable to think far enough ahead. It was the worker's job to help them.)

IMPLICATIONS FOR THE WORKER

In the cases so far discussed the worker was involved in one or other of two basic situations:

Situation One: The people or their representatives state a problem and seek the worker's advice as to how to meet it (e.g. Case 2,
Local Government)

Suggested Order of Work

1. Investigate with the people the exact nature of their problem.

2. Pool with them ideas as to possible solutions.

3. Encourage and help them to investigate the advantages *and* disadvantages of each with a view to deciding which solution is most acceptable and practical for them.

4. Leave the final decision entirely to them.

5. Help them to obtain any technical advice they may need while they are reaching their decision, or afterwards while they are implementing it.

Situation Two: The people or their representatives ask for help with a project they have chosen for themselves

(There is always a possibility that the people may have chosen a project that is unlikely to succeed because of adverse factors over which they have no control, but of which they are unaware as in Case 3, *The Brick Factory*; or because they have been influenced in their choice by status considerations as in Case 1, *The Unused Library*; or because they have not looked far enough ahead as in Case 4, *The Recreation Ground*. In all these cases the worker's problem is how to get the people to make a realistic reappraisal of what they have said they wanted to do, and to achieve this without sacrificing their goodwill.)

Suggested Order of Work

1. Draw attention to the relevant factors by asking questions such as, in the case of *The Unused Library*, 'Have you found out just how many people will actually join as subscribing members, and just what they want to read?'; or in the case of *The Brick Factory*, 'Have you been able to work out how much it will cost you to produce and market your bricks, and just who will buy them at a price that will enable you to pay your way?'

2. Involve the people themselves in getting the facts they need to enable them to answer such questions.

3. Encourage the people, if need be, to reconsider their existing plans in the light of the facts they have collected with a view to either

a. adapting them better to meet the requirements of their situation as they now see it; or

b. choosing a different project if they have reached the conclusion that their original project is impracticable or inappropriate.

Note on Working with 'Representative Committees'

Much of the worker's time is necessarily spent with small committees or groups which claim to represent the people but which do not always adequately reflect the aims and aspirations of the people they claim to represent. This faces the worker with a problem. One way of trying to deal with it is to get all major issues discussed and decisions taken at meetings open to everyone to attend, but this has its drawbacks as it is usually difficult to get a major issue fully discussed at a large meeting.

An alternative or additional method is to involve the members of the representative group in themselves systematically collecting from the people the information on which they can reach sound and informed decisions. This is the method suggested in the commentary to Case I, *The Unused Library*. It has the advantage that by thus involving the members of the committee in, as it were, checking on themselves, the worker also avoids the risk of antagonizing them by appearing to want to check on them himself.

CHAPTER THREE

Suggesting Community Projects

IN the cases described in the previous chapter the people themselves approached the worker to seek his help, but there are
many occasions on which it is the worker, not the people, who
first sees the need for change. He may then feel that it is his
duty to make the people aware of the need he sees, suggest what
they can do to meet it, and encourage them to act. Whether he
succeeds or fails will partly depend, of course, on whether the
people recognize the need as real, but partly also on other and
less obvious factors. Study of the cases which follow will reveal
some of these factors. In each case the worker failed because he
overlooked one or more of them.

5. PREVENTING FLOODS

The worker suggests that the people should agree to build a
river wall to prevent the periodic flooding of their homes and
crops. All they would have to give would be their labour, for
the government would provide all the rest. The people, however, though wanting to be free from floods, refuse to act.

THE CASE

I am an administrative officer. Most of the people in the district for
which I am responsible live in villages strung along the banks of a
big river. One of these villages is situated near the mouth of the river
where the level of the water rises and falls with the tides. In the wet
season the river is high between the banks, and when there is an
exceptionally high tide the river waters then overflow the banks and
flood into the village and over the surrounding farms. These floods
not only do a great deal of damage to the people's homes and farms,

but also to the main highway which connects all the villages on one bank of the river to the principal town of the district.

Since the central government is responsible for maintaining the road, it decided to build a concrete river wall to save it from being flooded. This solved the problem as far as the road was concerned, but it still left many of the village houses and farms quite unprotected. I therefore suggested to the villagers that they should apply for aid under the self-help scheme to extend the wall in both directions far enough to protect the remaining parts of the village. Under the self-help scheme all they would have to do would be to supply the labour. The central government would provide the technical supervision and all the necessary materials free.

The people, however, would not agree to this at all. Those who lived nearest to the road were not interested in the project because their homes and farms were already protected by the new wall. The others, the majority, whose homes were still liable to flooding, wanted the wall extended of course, but they wanted the central government to do it, just as it had already done the part that protected the road. I told them that the government could not afford to do this, for if it did it for them then people in other villages would want it too, but nothing I said made any impression on them. In the end I gave up trying. The wall has still not been extended and the people still suffer from the floods.

Diagnosis
DISCUSSION OF THE CASE

The members of the group which discussed this case felt that under the circumstances this administrative officer was almost bound to fail. His difficulties were caused, they thought, by the fact that the central government had already built a river wall to protect the road which also, though quite incidentally, had protected some of the people's homes and farms as well. The effect of this was to divide the village community into two groups: those whose homes and farms were now protected and who therefore were no longer worried by the flooding problem; and those who now felt badly treated because the central government, while protecting the homes and farms of others, had left theirs unprotected. Thus neither group was in a frame of mind to welcome the district officer's suggestion: the one, because its members were no longer subject to the danger of flooding; the other, because its members felt that the central government had a moral duty to protect them too. Also, even if the members of the latter group had reluctantly felt that it was in their own self-interest to work, they would have had to recognize that they would probably have to tackle the job without much help from those who were already safe from the danger of flooding.

Implications

In the light of this diagnosis the members of the group discussing the case went on to consider whether there were any alternatives which held out some hope of success. A few of them—those who had come from countries with a tradition of authoritarian rule—thought that the solution was clear. All that was needed, they said, was that the government should use its authority to force the people to labour on the wall. Since the project was designed solely to benefit them, once the wall was finished they would realize how useful it was and be glad that they were made to do the work.

Other members of the group disagreed strongly with this suggestion, partly because they had no power in their own countries to force people to work without pay; partly because they thought that by doing so they would worsen relations between themselves and the people; and partly because they thought that the project could have had a good chance of success if only the district officer had made his suggestion at an earlier and more favourable time. Going back to their diagnosis that the main cause of the problem was that the government had already protected the road, they suggested that if the officer had approached the people *before* this action had been taken, he would have had a much easier task: and that it would have been easier still if he had picked a time when the village had just been flooded. Everyone would then have had the evils of flooding in the forefront of his mind; no one would have felt safe from further flooding; and no one would have felt that he had been treated unfairly. Thus the chances of the people being willing to take action *as a community* would have been much enhanced, especially as the government could have offered generous help because of its own interest in protecting the road.

This second alternative looks as though it might have had a good chance of success. Why then was it not adopted? One reason, of course, is that the district officer did not think of it until after the wall to protect the road had been built. But this in turn may have been due to another reason—the lack of properly co-ordinated thinking and planning between the district administrative officer and the officer responsible for the maintenance of roads. In fact, neither seems to have realized that government action in protecting the road would adversely affect the people's willingness to extend the wall to protect themselves, and that they might get better results for the people of the area (and for the central government) by consulting and planning together rather than by working apart.

6. ERADICATING MOSQUITOES

The worker suggests to the people how they could stop malarial mosquitoes breeding in their village. The villagers enthusiastically agree with his suggestion, but only a few people turn out on the day fixed for the work to start.

THE CASE

I was trained as a village level worker. After completing my training I was posted to a rural area containing several villages. I was expected to work in all of them, but I lived in the largest village which was conveniently situated in the middle of my area. As I was very interested to get to know the people and their problems I travelled round the area a good deal, and one problem very quickly stood out above all others. Everywhere there were many mosquitoes which made life miserable for everyone. Also, many people suffered from malaria.

I noticed that in each of the villages there were several shallow pits from which the people were in the habit of taking the earth they used for building or repairing their houses. These were full of stagnant water during the rainy season and it was in this water that the mosquitoes were breeding. One of the first things I did, therefore, was to ask the headman of the village in which I lived to call a village meeting. At this meeting I explained that the mosquitoes were breeding in the pits and that the mosquitoes caused malaria (which the people already knew): and then suggested that they could get rid of most of the mosquitoes if they would fill in the pits. This the villagers at the meeting enthusiastically agreed to do, and a day was fixed for the work to begin as soon as the harvest was over.

That night I dreamt about the village with all the pits filled in and looked forward to the day when I would be able to sleep without a mosquito net. On the day the work was due to begin, however, only a very few people came, and none of the village leaders was among them. What had I done wrong? Or what hadn't I done that I ought to have done?

DISCUSSION OF THE CASE

Diagnosis

The group which discussed this case felt that any of several reasons might have caused the worker to fail. One reason suggested was that the people were not convinced that the mosquitoes really bred in the pits, or that they caused malaria, but others pointed out that we are told in the case that the people already knew this. The members of the group then went on to consider other possible causes and agreed on two as being the most likely.

The first of these was that although the worker was probably right in assuming that the people wanted to get rid of the mosquitoes, he was not therefore equally justified in assuming that they would readily accept his idea of filling in the pits as a solution to their problem. After all, even if they were convinced that the mosquitoes bred in the pits—and the worker seems to have expected them to take his word for it—they might reasonably suspect that the mosquitoes also bred in many other places as well. If so, they might well think it foolish to go to the trouble of filling in the pits if at the end of all their work there were still many mosquitoes to plague them.

Secondly, members of the group thought, even if the people believed that they really could get rid of all their mosquitoes by filling in the pits, it was still unlikely that they would fill them in: partly because of the immense amount of work that such a project would involve, but partly also because of the new problems it would create. Thus to fill in the pits the people would obviously have to use great quantities of earth. Where was this earth to be obtained unless the people dug new pits in which water was also likely to collect and mosquitoes breed? Again, even if this problem were solved and all the pits filled in, the people would still need clay to repair their existing houses and build new ones. How were they to get this clay in future without either making new pits or reopening old ones? The members of the group felt that although the worker seemed quite unaware of these practical difficulties, at least some members of the community must have been aware of them, and that this would amply explain why the people did not turn out on the day the work was due to start.

If, like the members of the group, one accepts these reasons as the likely explanation of why the project failed, how then can one explain the people's enthusiastic agreement with the worker's plan when he put it to them at the village meeting? The members of the group felt that this could be very simply explained in either of two ways. In very many village communities, they said, people are naturally polite, desirous to please, and anxious to avoid giving offence, especially where government officers are concerned. Such people would be likely to agree to the project, even if they had no intention of actually working on it when the time came, in order to avoid an immediate unpleasant situation and in the hope that by the time the harvest was over and work due to start the worker might have forgotten about it, or have changed his mind, or have been transferred to worry people somewhere else. Alternatively, they thought, the people might have agreed because they were genuinely enthusiastic about the project when the worker talked about it at the meeting, but that they changed their minds afterwards when they had time to talk it over among themselves and realize all the disadvantages it would entail.

Implications

In brief, then, the members of the group felt that the people had behaved very sensibly in rejecting the worker's proposal, both because it was inadequate, since at best it could only alleviate, not solve the problem, and impracticable since it did not take into account the people's continuing need for a local source of good building clay. Thus in the group's view the worker had only himself to blame for his failure.

Nevertheless, the group were agreed that the problem was a real one and that the worker had been right in trying to do something about it, even though what he actually did was wrong. So the task now facing the group was to suggest a more effective and acceptable solution.

All the members of the group felt that it might be very difficult to get the people to do anything, if only because they had had to live with mosquitoes all their lives and would need a lot of convincing that they could really do anything to get rid of them. The worker's best hope, the group thought, would be (*a*) to emphasize the discomfort and illness the mosquitoes caused; (*b*) to demonstrate very clearly and convincingly how they bred in stagnant water; and (*c*) to get the people to list, in the light of this knowledge, all the likely breeding places in their village. He could then, in relation to each kind of breeding place, help and encourage the people to think of practicable ways and means of preventing mosquitoes breeding in such places in the future, always with the emphasis on finding the simplest and easiest way. If he had done this, the effect would have been to educate the people to think of the whole problem —that of mosquitoes breeding anywhere in the village—and to find really acceptable and practicable methods of control, including keeping the village clear of broken pots, etc., in which water might collect. Had the problem of controlling breeding in the pits been discussed in this context, the group thought, the worker would have quickly realized that the people were more likely to agree for example to oil the surface of the water in the pits than to fill the pits in. Although this oiling would have had to be done regularly during the wet season (and hence the worker would need to get the people to decide just how they would ensure that this was done), it would be cheap and easy to do, and the people would still have convenient access to the clay they needed.

Having agreed that this was how they would choose to approach the problem, the members of the group now also agreed that they thought its solution would take a long time. This was because it could not be solved by getting the people to act together on a community project at any one time, but only by educating people to understand what they needed to do, both as individuals and as a community, day by day and year by year to prevent mosquitoes breeding in their village.

7. MAKING-UP THE ROAD

The worker suggests to a community of rice farmers that they should put into good order the muddy, pot-holed track that runs between their houses. The people agree and do a good deal of work but do not complete it.

THE CASE

I am an administrative officer and I encountered the difficulty I am about to describe when I tried to get the people of a newly-settled community of rice-farmers to make up the road along which their houses were situated. This was still no more than a muddy track and during the wet season it was quite impassable except on foot. It was only about a mile long and the people's houses—some sixty of them—were on scattered plots along its entire length. At the end of the track was the main road which led to the outside world.

At first all went well. I called a public meeting of all the settlers and put my suggestions to them. I explained that the project would involve making a drain along the length of the road to carry off rainwater; levelling the inequalities of the existing track; and then giving it a good hard surface that would not turn into mud during the rains. I said I could get them all the technical advice they needed if only they would take full responsibility for actually carrying out the work. This they readily agreed to undertake. They were busy on their farms during the week, they said, but they had Sundays free and they would work each week-end until the project had been properly completed.

During the first three months they made very good progress. I sent out a Public Works foreman to help them mark out the line for the drain and this was quickly dug. Then they levelled the road and started surfacing it, starting from where the track joined the main road. It was then that the trouble began for they made only slow progress and many of them seemed to lose heart. They started grumbling and some of them even suggested that I ought to get Government to come in to finish the job. Also some of the settlers—those who lived nearest to the main road—refused to go on working because the road had already been surfaced beyond the point at which their own houses were situated and they saw no benefit for themselves in completing the road for the benefit of the others. I did my best to get the people to make one big final effort to finish the job but they would not listen. In the end they gave up the project without ever surfacing the last two-thirds of the road, and this part of the road is now just as bad as it ever was. I was disappointed naturally, but also quite a bit worried, for the failure of the project has caused a lot of bad feeling in the village between the people who live nearest to the main road and those who live farthest away from the part of the road which was finished.

DISCUSSION OF THE CASE

Diagnosis

The group which discussed this case felt that the worker's choice of project was sound enough in the sense that *if* the people had completed it it would have met a real need. Where the worker went wrong, the group felt, was in too readily assuming that the people's enthusiasm would last until the project was completed. As the case shows, this assumption was quite unjustified, and members of the group thought that the worker could have anticipated the possibility of trouble—and taken steps to guard against it—if he had thought out in some detail just how much work per household the project was likely to involve and just what were the chances that the settlers would be able to finish it in view of all the other work they had to do.

The hardest part of the project, the group thought, was the surfacing of the road: for while neither the digging of a drain nor the levelling of the road would involve much carrying of earth, to surface the road properly would almost certainly

involve carrying a very heavy weight of road metal from wherever it could be found. In a rice-growing area this was unlikely
to be found near at hand, and thus one reason for the failure,
in the opinion of the group, was that the people found the
work of surfacing the road much heavier than they had anticipated when, in the first flush of enthusiasm, they had agreed to
the project.

The members of the group felt that this factor was all the
more significant in view of the fact that the community was a
small one of only sixty households and entirely composed of
new settlers who, as the case tells us, were already so busy on
their farms that they were free to work on the road for only one
day (the Sunday) of each week. This meant that the project
would take many weeks to complete, and that during the whole
of that time the people would be continuously at work, on their
farms or on the road, without a rest-day of any kind. All things
considered, members of the group felt, it was not surprising
that the people got tired.

Even so, since the settlers really wanted the road and did in
fact do a great deal of work on it, the group thought that the
worker might still have had a chance of getting the people to
finish it if they had not started surfacing the road from the main
road end. This had the effect of splitting the community for, as
we are told in the case, the settlers who lived nearest to the main
road lost interest in the project when the road had been completed as far as their own house lot and ceased to do any more
work. It was when this happened that the others finally lost heart.

Implications

The members of the group then discussed the implications
of their diagnosis for the worker. Although the project had
failed, they still thought that it was potentially a good and useful one, that the worker was right in suggesting it, and that if
he had been more careful it could have had a good chance of
success. In particular, they felt that he should have done much
more to get the people to think out how much work they would
have to do (*a*) to dig a mile of drainage ditch; (*b*) to level the

mile-long stretch of track; and (c) to surface it. He could have done this by asking questions which would have got them thinking quite concretely about how many days they would each have to work on digging, levelling and surfacing: and, in connexion with the surfacing, where suitable surfacing material could be got, at what distance from the road, and in what quantity it would be needed. His purpose in asking such questions would be to temper their enthusiasm with realism so that if they decided to tackle the project they would know in advance just what sacrifices, in terms of weeks of Sunday work, they would each have to make, and just how long it would take before the project was completed.

If the worker had got the people to think in this realistic way, the group thought, it was quite possible that the settlers might reluctantly have decided to abandon the project; or, alternatively, to delay starting work on it until such time as they were less busy on their farms and could devote more days a week to it. Either of these results, the group felt, would have been more satisfactory than what actually happened in the case. If on the other hand the settlers decided to go ahead with the project in spite of all the difficulties they could now envisage, they would be much more likely to continue working until they had brought the project to a satisfactory conclusion.

The group also felt very strongly that the worker might reasonably have been able to foresee the adverse effect that the surfacing of the road from the main road end was likely to have on the willingness of the settlers living at the end of the road to continue working once the road had been surfaced as far as their own houses. Had the worker pointed this out to the settlers when they were planning the project, the group thought that they would quickly have recognized the danger and taken steps to avoid it. This they could have done quite easily had they decided to surface that part of the track nearest to the main road last. It was the worker's failure to alert the settlers to this danger, some members of the group felt, more than to any other of his omissions, that the final failure of the project was mainly due.

8. THE WANT THAT WASN'T FELT

The worker gets the people to build themselves a community centre, but finds out later that what they really wanted was a road.

THE CASE

Recently the government of my country introduced a scheme to encourage village people to undertake local projects to improve their communities. Under this scheme the administrative officer in charge of each district was empowered to make a grant to cover the cost of the materials needed for a project if he thought the project was a good one, and if the people were willing to give their labour free.

I am a district administrative officer. Soon after this scheme had been approved, I noted that the people of a certain village had no proper place in which to meet. So I explained the scheme to them and suggested that they might like to build a community centre as a project under the scheme. The people agreed, a plan was decided on, and I arranged for the necessary materials to be delivered to the site.

The people then started work, but the building of the centre made very slow progress. Only a few of the younger people showed any real interest. The rest, including all the older people, soon stopped doing any work at all.

The community centre was still only half-finished when the people sent in an application for a second grant—this time for a road on which they said they would all be willing to work as they needed it very badly. I was now in a quandary, for if I approved the scheme for the road I was sure that the centre would never be finished, and that the materials I had sent would either be stolen or left to rot on the site. I therefore refused a grant for the road until the centre was finished, and in the end the people did finish it, but even now they've got their centre completed they don't use it. What's wrong with them?

Diagnosis

The group which discussed this case suggested several reasons to account for what happened. On the assumption that the people agreed to build the centre because they wanted it, some members suggested that perhaps the people had made the mistake of planning the centre on too ambitious a scale and only realized how big a job they had undertaken after they had started work, whereupon they lost heart. Others thought that the people might have been so divided among themselves by faction differences that they would have been unable to work happily together on any project. Others, again, thought that the timing of the project may have been at fault. If work on the project had coincided with the busy season on the farms, or with an election, or with some other happening, this might have been quite enough to explain the slow progress with the building of the centre.

None of these reasons, however, seemed to fit in well enough with all the facts in the case, and soon all the members of the group felt pretty well agreed that the most likely explanation was that the people, at any rate most of the people, neither wanted a centre nor had they any clear idea what use they could make of a centre if they had one. This, the members of the group felt, was the only way they could account for the people wanting to abandon the community centre project in favour of a road project, and also for them not making use of the centre when they had finally finished building it.

But if the people had no use for a centre, why then did they agree to build it in the first place? The group thought there were two possible answers to this question: one, that the people agreed because they were in the habit of doing what their administrative officer told them to do, and because they felt it was in their own interest to do what pleased him; and the other, that they may have thought that by building a community centre they would raise their status *vis-à-vis* the people of the neighbouring villages. The group also thought that the people probably only realized the full extent of what they had let themselves in for after they had started work: and that they then decided that if they were going to work on a project they would much rather work for a road, which they really wanted, than for the community centre their administrative officer had suggested. Hence their own (spontaneous) application for a grant for building a road.

Implications

The members of the group then went on to discuss what the administrative officer might alternatively have done. Most members felt that he should have started by explaining the self-help scheme, and then asking the people what project, if any, they would like to undertake. This would have left them free to think for themselves and to suggest whatever project they liked. This would have probably been a road. Once he was sure that this was what they really wanted; that they all realized just how much they themselves would have to do; and that they had both the will and the resources to complete it, he could then quite safely have used his powers under the self-help scheme to help them. Had he acted in this way, the group thought, he would have saved himself a great deal of worry and trouble, and the people a great deal of wasted effort.

CONCLUSIONS

Study of the cases included in this chapter suggests the following conclusions:

1. *The worker should not assume, because the people readily agree to the project he suggests, that they therefore want it and will genuinely do their best to carry it through to a successful conclusion.*

(In Case 6, *Eradicating Mosquitoes*, for instance, the people's enthusiastic agreement appears to have meant no more than that they wanted to please the worker: but they changed their minds later on when they had had more time to think about the project and realize more clearly all its implications for themselves. In Case 7, *Making-up the Road*, the people's agreement was more genuine. They appear to have really wanted the road and to be willing to work for it. The worker, however, did little or nothing to help them realize just how much work they would have to do, and when they found that the surfacing of the road was a much bigger job than they had expected they gave up. In Case 8, *The Want that Wasn't Felt*, on the other hand, the people's agreement was entirely misleading for they seem to have been willing to agree to almost anything the worker suggested solely because they were so much in the habit of deferring to authority. This, however, did not prevent them from trying to abandon the project afterwards.

In all these cases, one feels, the worker would have done much better if only he had taken enough trouble to get the people to weigh up realistically all the pros and cons of the project he suggested, while leaving them quite free to decide for themselves whether they really wanted to undertake it or not. (If the people had then decided to accept it, it is far more likely that they would have completed it and benefited from it. On the other hand, if they had rejected it, surely this would have been better than that they should agree to it and then change their minds as in Case 6, *Eradicating Mosquitoes*; or start on it and then abandon it as in Case 7, *Making-up the Road*; or, having finished it, find they have no real use for it as in Case 8, *The Want that Wasn't Felt.*)

2. *The worker must try to ensure that the project has and will retain the support of everyone whose help is needed.*

(The main reason why the worker failed to get community support for the flood protection scheme he suggested in Case 5, *Preventing Floods*, was that some of the people had already been protected by the government-built wall. Had he suggested the project earlier, when everyone was subject to flooding, he would have had a much better chance of success. The same factor also contributed to the worker's failure in Case 7, *Making-up the Road*, when, during the course of the project, some of the settlers lost interest when the road was completed as far as their own house lot. In both of these cases the worker might have succeeded if he had been aware of this factor and planned his work accordingly.)

IMPLICATIONS FOR THE WORKER

Situation: The worker wants to suggest a specific project for community action

Suggested Order of Work

A. *Before suggesting the project*

1. Define for oneself as clearly and specifically as possible the exact need or needs one hopes the project will meet. (This the worker failed to do in Case 8, *The Want that Wasn't Felt.*)

2. Consider whether the project will benefit everyone or some people only. If the latter, consider whether it is suitable for launching as a *community* project. (This the worker did not do in Case 5, *Preventing Floods*.)

3. Check to make as sure as one can that the project one intends to suggest is well designed to meet the need that one sees (e.g. that it is not only technically sound, but also practicable in relation to the local environment and the skills and resources locally available).

4. Assess as precisely as one can the *disadvantages* of the project for the people (e.g. its demands on scarce resources and on people's leisure, both while the project is being implemented and afterwards).

5. Assess as precisely as one can the actual *balance of advantage* as the people are likely to view it. (This the worker did not do in Case 6, *Eradicating Mosquitoes*, and in Case 8, *The Want that Wasn't Felt*.)

6. If the balance of advantage appears to be unfavourable— that is, if one feels that one would oneself probably reject the project if one were a member of the community—then consider how one can amend the project in order to reduce the disadvantages.

7. Delay introducing the project until one feels that one can introduce it with at least a fair chance of success.

B. *When suggesting the project*

1. First ask whether the need (see item 1 above) exists, and promote discussion with a view to getting the people to assess it for themselves.

2. If the people confirm that they have such a need, *tentatively* propose the project as a possible means of meeting the need, stressing both the advantages that could be anticipated if the project were successfully completed *and* that some disadvantages might also be entailed.

3. Promote discussion with a view to getting the people to assess
    (*a*) the extent of the benefits that the project would bring;
    (*b*) how practicable it would be for them in relation to their local situation, skills and resources; and

(c) just what difficulties and disadvantages they would need to anticipate.

4. Promote discussion to see whether and to what extent the people think these difficulties and disadvantages could be overcome.

5. Suggest any other difficulties or disadvantages, immediate or future, which one fears might endanger the success of the project, but which the people have so far overlooked.

6. Promote discussion as to how far these are real, and as to how they can be avoided or overcome.

7. Promote discussion with a view to getting the people to decide for or against the project as amended in the light of the previous discussions.

8. If the people decide in favour
(a) encourage and help them to plan the project in the light of all the factors previously discussed.
(b) help them to obtain any technical advice or help they may need.

Note on the Advantages and Disadvantages of following this Procedure

Advantages

1. If the people do decide to accept the project, they are then far more likely to complete it and make good use of it than if the worker merely tries to 'sell' it to them on the advantages he sees.

2. He increases the people's confidence in him as someone who really is trying to help them, rather than trying to get them to do what he or his agency wants them to do.

3. He does not 'lose face' with the people if they decide against the project.

Disadvantages

The disadvantage is that the worker runs a rather greater risk that the people may decide against the project. This disadvantage, however, is more apparent than real, since if the balance of advantage actually is unfavourable, the people are liable to reject it sooner or later anyway, as they did in all the cases included in this chapter.

D

CHAPTER FOUR

Introducing Improvements

THE encouragement of community projects is one way of promoting community betterment, but not the only one. Thus, while people may agree to work together on some specific community project in order, for instance, to provide themselves with some needed community amenity such as a road, a school, a clean water-supply, or a community centre, they may have many other needs which they cannot meet merely by working in this way. Such needs, for example, may be to improve their homes, or their methods of agriculture, or their diet, or the way they bring up their children: and to help them to meet these needs the worker may have to try to educate and stimulate them to implement changes of many kinds.

This is difficult work, for it may involve getting many individuals to accept major changes in habit or custom for reasons which they do not initially understand, and which the worker therefore has to be able to make clear. Also, his task will be still more difficult, as some of the following cases will show, if the people think they have some reason to suspect his motives.

9. HELPING THE FARMERS

The worker tries to get farmers to agree to a scheme for redistributing and consolidating their holdings, but they refuse.

THE CASE

The holdings of most of the farmers in a newly-established development area were too small and too badly fragmented to provide them with a decent livelihood. It was therefore decided to make available to them some additional land on condition that they all agreed to give up their scattered plots for reallocation into larger individual compact holdings.

As I was the development officer in that area I had the job of introducing the plan, which I did at a meeting of the Development Area Council on which the farmers were represented. I pointed out to the members of the council that if the farmers accepted the plan they would benefit in many ways. They would have more land. They would no longer have to waste time in going from one small plot to another. They would find a compact farm easier to drain and fence. They could also make good use of tractors.

I then called a meeting of all the farmers, but although I took great pains to explain the plan's advantages very carefully, no one showed any enthusiasm for it. As a follow-up, therefore, I asked several of the most influential of the farmers to see me individually in my office in the hope that if only I could convince them they in turn would help to convince others. But I failed with them also. They had, they said, farmed their existing lands for years and they intended to go on farming them. They knew exactly what they could produce. As for the new scheme, who knew what land he would get or what kind of soil?

And so in the end I had to abandon the scheme. Was it bound to fail or might I have had a better chance of success if I had approached the problem differently?

DISCUSSION OF THE CASE

Diagnosis

The officers who discussed this case all felt that the idea behind the scheme was a good one and likely to have benefited the farmers, if only they had accepted it. Asked why they thought the farmers refused to accept it, they were able to think of quite a number of reasons. Some thought that perhaps the worker had been responsible for introducing some previous scheme affecting the farmers in this area, and that this earlier scheme had failed with bad results for the farmers. If this were so, it might have so weakened their confidence in the development officer that they would be mistrustful of any other changes he proposed. Others thought that he was so obsessed by the advantages of the scheme, as he saw them, that he was quite unable to realize that the farmers, viewing it from their angle, might have very good reasons for hesitating before they agreed to commit themselves to it. Farmers everywhere, they said, are very attached to their land and they could not imagine farmers anywhere agreeing to part with their existing holdings which they knew, for the promise of a larger holding the site of which had yet to be determined. Others, while agreeing that this was likely to be a major source of difficulty, felt that it might have been surmounted if the farmers had been invited to discuss and agree among themselves how the boundaries of the proposed consolidated holdings should be fixed and the holdings allocated. Others, again, felt that it was unrealistic to attempt to introduce such a scheme for the whole of the area, and that the chances of success would have been greatly increased if the development officer had contented himself initially with trying to introduce a small pilot scheme affecting only a minority of the farmers. Some thought also that he may have been wrong in introducing the scheme at a meeting of the Development Area Council instead of discussing it with the farmers to find out what they thought about it first.

After these points had been further discussed, the members of the group all felt that in trying to sell the scheme by stressing only its advantages, the development officer had contributed very significantly to his own failure. At no time did he show any real understanding of the viewpoint of the farmers. All that weighed with him were the *general* advantages he expected the scheme to bring to all the farmers in the area, while what mattered to the farmers were their own individual assessment of all its possible effects on them. From each of these individual viewpoints the scheme looked much less attractive. It presented each farmer with one certainty—that he would have to give up the land he knew, and to which, like peasant farmers everywhere, he felt deeply attached: and with one uncertainty—whether he would get equally good and acceptable land back in return. While this uncertainty remained, each farmer could feel, and did feel, that the exchange after all might turn out badly for him—poor land in exchange for good, for instance, or land situated inconveniently far from his home. This was a risk no farmer was willing to take, and it was this, almost certainly, that caused the scheme to fail. It was also the one factor that the development officer did not take into account. In his meeting with the Development Area Council and in his subsequent meetings with the farmers he appears to have concentrated solely on stressing the scheme's quite obvious advantages, and at no time does he show any real understanding of the individual farmer's point of view.

Implications

If this diagnosis is correct the development officer would have increased his chances of success if, instead of trying to 'sell' the scheme by stressing only its advantages, he had put it forward as an idea the pros and cons of which the farmers might find it worth while to discuss. He would then have stated what the government was prepared to do (i.e. make some additional land available), and the condition they would impose (that the farmers would agree to consolidate their holdings), and ask the farmers for their reactions. In the ensuing discussions he would have quickly discovered whether the farmers did indeed want a better livelihood—the supposition on which the whole idea of the scheme was based. If they really did not want it—if they were quite content to go on as they were—then the most sensible thing to have done would have been to drop the scheme until their attitude had changed: and since he had not openly committed himself to the scheme by trying to sell it, he could easily have done this without loss of face. If, however, as seems more likely, the farmers were interested in getting a better livelihood, but opposed the scheme because each felt he might receive an inconvenient or inferior plot, the development officer could then have proceeded to explore with them how, if at all, this difficulty could be overcome. He might have asked, for instance, if the farmers would like to view the additional land in order to assess its soil for themselves. He might also have asked if they would feel happier about the scheme if they chose their own representatives to fix the boundaries of the proposed new holdings, and if, when these had been agreed on, a ballot were held to decide on how the holdings should be allocated. And if, after these and other points had been discussed, some farmers were for and some against the scheme, he might then have suggested that those in favour might decide to co-operate in a smaller pilot scheme.

If the development officer had done all this he would still have had no certainty of success, but he would have made success more likely, and even if he had failed he would still have improved his standing with the people. By putting the scheme forward without trying to press the farmers into accepting it against their own judgement; by exploring both its advantages and disadvantages with them; and by trying to help them see whether its disadvantages could in any way be overcome, he would have demonstrated in the clearest possible way his genuine desire to help them. At the same time he would have thereby created a situation in which the true merits of the scheme would have been more realistically and objectively assessed.

10. THE BEE EXPERT

A community development officer tries to get people to start keeping bees for the profit they could get from the honey and wax, but they mistrust his intentions and refuse to co-operate.

THE CASE

I am a community development officer, and at the time I encountered the problem outlined in this case I was in charge of an extension team in a small development area consisting of some eleven villages.

We, the members of the team and I, had visited the area several times before starting work. We did this partly in order to win the people's confidence and partly in order to study their needs. As a result of these visits I decided to concentrate mainly on helping the men to build new or better villages—which was what they said they wanted—and to help the women by teaching them simple ideas about how to improve their homes.

After about a month on the job we had a meeting of the team to evaluate what we had already done, and to plan our work for the month that lay ahead. At this meeting one of the members of the team suggested that we ought to recruit a bee expert. Such a man, he thought, would be very useful since there were many flowering trees in the area and many bees: while the local people did nothing to make use of them except to collect a little wild honey by waste-fully destroying the nests the bees had made. If they were taught how to make hives, collect the honey properly, and make beeswax, he said, not only would they get a great deal of honey, but they would also get a cash income from the sale of the wax.

We all thought this was a very good idea and soon afterwards I managed to get a bee-man attached to the team. I introduced him to the people in the villages and explained what he could do to help them. They listened quite politely, but no one showed any interest at all. However, I decided to go ahead and set the bee-man to work making bark hives and putting them in the trees. But every time a hive was put into a tree the next day we found it lying smashed up on the ground. I did my best to get the people to change their attitude, but nothing I could do had the slightest effect. Somehow they had convinced themselves that all we were after was to give Government an excuse for increasing their tax, either by putting a tax on the trees, or on the wax, or on the people who owned the hives. In the end I gave up trying and sent the bee-man away.

DISCUSSION OF THE CASE
Diagnosis

The members of the group which discussed this case agreed that mistrust of government intentions was a very common source of difficulty for community workers, and that the case they were about to discuss was a typical example of the kind of difficulty that often occurred. They then divided into sub-groups to discuss it. When they returned to pool their ideas in the full group they found that their main point, on which they were all agreed, was that the leader of the team should not have brought in the bee-man without first consulting the people. What he had done was to present the people with a *fait accompli* for which he had in no way prepared them and which to them seemed to have no very clear and obvious connexion with the other activities of the team in the area. In view of the people's existing predisposition to mistrust, the group felt, this was just the kind of approach most likely to give rise to the adverse rumour and speculation which had actually occurred.

Apart from this, however, the members of the group felt that the leader's approach would have been open to criticism even if the situation had been much more favourable than it actually was. It was clear that he thought the project a good one, but what really mattered was what the people thought, for everything would depend on how willing they were to co-operate in making the project a success: and it would have been much better if he had not openly committed himself to it while the people's response was still in doubt. Thus the group felt that he might reasonably have expected to have to answer many questions and clear up many doubts. It was not enough that he should believe that the scheme would be profitable. The people would want to know *how* profitable, and at what cost in time and labour to themselves. They might need to be convinced that the bees would actually enter the hives if they made them, and that they would actually get enough honey to compensate them for the extra work involved. They would also want to know what they would have to do to prepare the wax for market, where they could sell it, and at what price. They might also have very sound reasons, based on their own past experience, for suspecting that their taxes might go up if they made a success of the project. On the whole, the group thought, the people were right to be cautious until they had been reassured on all these points even if they were not, as they were in this case, already actively mistrustful.

Some members of the group, while agreeing with all that has been written above, thought that some other reason must also have been present to account for the actual destruction of the bee-man's hives. One such reason, they thought, might be that the bee-man himself was disliked, either because he belonged to a different and unpopular tribe or because of something he had done after he had arrived. It was equally possible that the people had strongly resented him placing his hives in their trees without their express permission.

Implications

The group then went on to consider more specifically what the leader should alternatively have done. Everyone felt that he should have thought out much more specifically right from the beginning just what doubts the people were likely to have about the scheme, and just what he would need to do in order to set these doubts at rest. He should then have suggested the idea as something the people might like to consider. He should have outlined the advantages as he saw them, and also the snags, and then invited the people to discuss it among themselves and with him until they had made up their minds one way or the other. If the people showed signs of becoming interested and asked specific technical questions about how hives were made or beeswax prepared which he could not answer himself, he could then have suggested that he would, if they wished, try to get a knowledgeable bee-man to come and demonstrate how these things should be done. He could also say that if the people still wished to go ahead with the project after the demonstrations, he would try to get the bee-man attached to the team. Had he made his approach along these lines, the members of the group thought, most of his difficulties would have disappeared. The people would have been much less suspicious because they would not now feel that the worker was trying to impose the project on them, and they would have found it much easier openly to voice their fears, e.g. about the possibility of increased taxation. The worker could then have tried to find out for them how far such fears were well-founded. Also, if the people did become attracted to the idea, he would have put them in the position of themselves asking for a bee-man to be appointed to the team. This in itself would be the best possible guarantee they would be likely to co-operate with him once he was appointed.

11. THE CASSAVA GRATERS

As a first step towards the introduction of cassava-grating machines in a rural area the worker is told to find out how many women are at present engaged in preparing cassava for sale by hand. He runs into difficulty when the people become suspicious of his intentions.

THE CASE

The government of my country is anxious to encourage small rural industries. As a part of this policy it was decided to try to get the women in the area in which I am posted to form small co-operative groups to buy and operate a new kind of machine for grating cassava, instead of grating it by hand as heretofore.

I was told, however, that I must not go ahead with forming these co-operative groups until I had first found out how many women were at present preparing cassava for sale by hand, and how many of them would be willing to organize themselves into groups in order to buy and work the machines. I was told to get this information quickly so that the Ministry would know in good time how many machines were likely to be needed.

I therefore went on tour at once, and at a series of village meetings I explained the scheme to the people and asked them to co-operate through their headman in providing me with the information I needed. Since they would wish to discuss the scheme among themselves, and this would take a little time, I told them I would come back again to collect this information in three weeks time. By the end of my tour I was feeling very happy. The women had seemed very interested in the scheme and I had been warmly welcomed everywhere I went.

On my second tour, however, everything was quite different. The people were sullen and the information I wanted was nowhere forthcoming. The reason, apparently, was that soon after my first visit a team of tax collectors carrying long lists of the names of tax defaulters had invaded the villages, and that many people had been arrested. Since I was asking for lists of names, the people were now suspecting that I was somehow in league with the tax collectors and would have nothing more to do with me. Was there anything that could have done to avoid this happening?

DISCUSSION OF THE CASE

Diagnosis

The group which discussed this case first considered whether the worker might reasonably have foreseen the possibility of trouble, and if so whether he could have done anything to prevent it. A few members thought that he might. They said that tax collection drives were quite common in some places and that in any one district it was likely to take place at about the same time each year. The worker could therefore have predicted that such a drive was about to take place if only he had thought it significant in connexion with the project. He could then have inquired at the tax office, and once he knew for certain he should have seen the tax officer with a view to getting the drive postponed.

Other members of the group, however, thought this altogether too much to expect of any worker. They thought, too, that even if he had approached the tax officer he would not have succeeded in getting him to alter his arrangements. As for the worker, certainly he could not afford to wait since his Ministry had told him he must get to work quickly.

This led some members of the group to remark rather bitterly that many of their most difficult problems were caused less by the people among whom they worked than by the unhelpful attitudes of their colleagues in other departments, and by their own ministries' demands for quick results. All too often the effect was to put the worker into a quite impossible situation.

Implications

The members of the group felt that their diagnosis had more relevance for the worker's Ministry than for the worker himself. In general, they felt that the officials of his Ministry should have left the worker much freer to plan and carry out the project. After all, he was in a much better position to judge how to tackle the people of his own local area than they were. Had they realized this, the group thought, the outcome of the project might have been very different. The worker would have been less pressed for time, and he would not have had to start, for example, by asking how many women in each village were already engaged in preparing cassava for sale: and it was this kind of question that had aroused the people's suspicion. Instead, he could have concentrated on demonstrating the new grating machine; getting the various advantages, and disadvantages of the project thoroughly discussed; investigating the chances of getting the women to agree to organize themselves into co-operative groups; and then getting a few groups established as a kind of pilot project. It was only when these had proved themselves so demonstrably successful that he could be sure that the project would catch on elsewhere that he would be able to submit a reasonably reliable estimate of the number of grating machines likely to be needed for his area as a whole.

Had he been able to start in this way, the group thought, he would have had quite a fair chance of success, for even if the tax collectors had been operating at the time there would have been nothing to connect him with them in the people's minds. Even so, had he known, or taken the trouble to find out, that the drive was about to take place, the members of the group thought that he would have been wise to delay starting on the project until the drive was over and any resentment it had aroused had died down.

12. CONSERVING THE SOIL

The worker manages to get the people to agree to a soil conservation scheme and put it into effect. Two years later, however, the people destroy most of the work already done and revert to their old ways.

THE CASE

In my district there is a hilly area which had been so heavily over-cultivated and over-grazed that it had become very badly eroded. Because of this my government sent a soil conservation officer to study the problem. He reported that the people must give up cultivating certain areas altogether so that they could be planted with trees; that during each summer they must send most of their flocks and herds out of the valley to graze high up on the hillsides; and that the people of some of the villages must move to new and approved sites. In addition he recommended that a team of technicians with heavy earth-moving equipment should be sent to the area to construct dams and other works at certain key points.

I had the job of getting this scheme accepted by the people of the area. I therefore first explained it to the District Council. This was the local authority for the whole of my district. Most of its members were chiefs and among them, of course, were the chiefs of the area affected by the scheme. This Council readily agreed to make and enforce whatever rules were needed to ensure the scheme's success.

I then went to the area where the scheme had to be applied. There I held several meetings to explain the scheme to the people. I stressed that it was designed to help them and that it was in their own interest for them to co-operate. I also told them that the scheme had the support of their District Council, and that the Council would be making regulations which would be enforced according to custom by their own chiefs. I was pleased with the results of these meetings, for the people quite readily agreed to support the scheme and also to obey whatever regulations the District Council might make in connexion with it.

The scheme had proceeded fairly satisfactorily for two years when it suddenly collapsed. The people just refused to co-operate any more, and some of them became so hostile that they actually destroyed some of the work already done. Eventually, the team had to be withdrawn, and although some of the people then said they would like the team to come back, none of them were willing to make any further sacrifices for the scheme themselves. Now the whole area is back in the state it was in before the scheme started. Could this failure have been avoided?

DISCUSSION OF THE CASE
Diagnosis

The members of the group which discussed this case first tried to understand why the people had changed their minds about a scheme which they had agreed to accept and which they had implemented for two whole years. After considerable discussion about why the people had accepted the scheme in the first place, the group thought that they had probably done so because

(*a*) they were probably already aware that soil erosion was taking place—we are told in the case that the area had become very badly eroded—and were therefore genuinely anxious that something should be done to safeguard their future on the land;

(*b*) in the process of 'selling' the scheme the worker had probably under-emphasized or ignored the many sacrifices they would have to make in order to implement it properly, thus making it appear more attractive than it really was;

(*c*) the worker had succeeded in getting the District Council, which was mainly composed of the people's own traditional rulers, to support the scheme; and this also influenced the people in favour of it. (This influence was all the more important, members of the group felt, because

from their reading of the case they inferred that the chief
in this area still had a great deal of influence and power.

As for the reasons why the scheme collapsed two years later
the members of the group thought that discontent must have
been building up gradually for a very long time as the people
slowly came to realize the full implications of all the sacrifice
they were having to make; that the scheme was only able to
continue for as long as it did because the people were subjected
to a great deal of administrative pressure channelled through
the chiefs; and that the worker was only able to remain unaware
for so long that serious trouble was brewing because, in view of
this pressure, the people had no very easy and obvious way of
voicing their complaints. Thus the worker pressed ahead with
the scheme while the people's resentment against it grew, until
at last the people felt they could bear it no longer and came out
in open revolt against it.

Implications

The group thought that the scheme's chances of success
might have been increased in two ways: the one, by an educational programme designed to bring home to the people, in the
clearest possible way, the danger of neglecting to take really
effective action to safeguard what remained of the fertility of
their soil; and the other, by inviting them to share in the planning of all those aspects of the scheme they would need to
implement themselves.

Before any attempt was made to plan the scheme as such, the
first thing that should have been done, members of the group
felt, was to get the chiefs, sub-chiefs, and some of the more
influential people in each of the villages interested in helping
the soil conservation officer to assess the nature and extent of
their soil erosion problem. This, the group thought, would have
been the best possible way of making the people of the area
fully aware of what was actually happening to their soil and of
how necessary it was that something should be done about it
quickly. This should have been followed by many local demonstrations, live or on film, of just what needed to be done. In all

his the aim would have been to create such an awareness of the
ature and urgency of the soil erosion problem that the people
hemselves would ask for the government's help in dealing
vith it.

This would have provided a very favourable climate for the
ctual planning of the scheme which, the group felt, should
ave been the outcome of consultation between the soil con-
ervation officer, the worker in charge of the area, and local
ommittees representative of the people. The technical officer
vould then have been in the position of being able to advise
he members of these committees about what he thought they
ught to do and why it was necessary. They could then have
iscussed his proposals with a view to deciding how they could
est put them into effect while reducing, if possible, some of
heir disadvantages to themselves. As they reached these
ecisions, so the scheme would take shape: and in its final form
t would then reflect, to the greatest possible extent, practicable
olutions to both the technical and human aspects of the problem.
he people would then have felt that the scheme was *their* scheme.
hey would have understood much better why the scheme was
ecessary, and would have realized that, having helped to plan
t, it was now up to them to do their best to carry it out.

Had the worker been free to tackle the problem in this way
nstead of having to try to sell a pre-fixed scheme to the people,
he group felt that his prospects of success would have been
reatly improved. But in fact he was not free. Again, had the
cheme been introduced before the area had become so badly
roded, he might have succeeded better because then the people
vould not have had to sacrifice quite so much. Given the actual
ircumstances of the case, however, the members of the group
hought he was almost bound to fail.

13. TURNING NOMADS INTO FARMERS

A rural extension worker encourages and helps a semi-
omadic community to settle down as farmers on the land. All
oes well for three years, but then he meets with total failure.

THE CASE

Until quite recently I was in charge of extension work at one of the rural development centres in my country. While I was doing this job I became very interested in a semi-nomadic community of some eighty shepherd families who were living in the hills about fifteen miles from the centre. Besides grazing their sheep they collected honey and firewood from the forest for sale in a nearby market. They were very poor, and their main contact with the outside world was their contact with the workers who visited them from our centre.

We became very friendly with these people and wished to help them, and I decided that the best way to do this was to try to settle them as farmers on the land. I explained to the shepherds what I had in mind for them and how useful the crops they could grow would be. They trusted me and willingly agreed to do whatever we required of them. I then posted a good worker to work with that community and in due course, and with some help from the centre, three hundred acres of forest land were cleared and prepared for the sowing of crops.

For the first three years all went well and I was very proud of this project. Even Ministers were among the many visitors who came to see that place and they praised me with loud words. During the whole of that time the shepherds did whatever we asked them to do, although they never showed any initiative themselves. We were not much worried by this because we thought that they would get used to the agricultural way of life in the course of time.

Then came the year of the rice crop. Nice green sprouts of the rice plants came up in the fields for the first time in history and my heart was full of joy and pride.

Then one day our worker came from the village with the shocking news that the shepherds had let loose their sheep in the field at night, that all the crop was destroyed, and that all the men had run away from their village taking their sheep with them. They did not return for many days. We had to bring our worker back to the centre and abandon the project. We were distressed and puzzled by our failure. After all, the project had gone on well for three whole years.

DISCUSSION OF THE CASE

Diagnosis

The members of the group which discussed this case felt that they could only explain it in terms of a long succession of unanticipated difficulties and frustrations which the people tried hard to tolerate because they liked and trusted the extension worker, but which finally became too much for them so that in the end they gave up like a dam that suddenly collapses after a long time under an intolerable weight of water. What these difficulties were the members of the group could only guess, but they suggested that some of them might be:

1. that the people had formerly enjoyed a relatively free and leisurely way of life which came to an end once they had started work on the project;

2. that the project had an adverse effect on the people's other economic activities, such as grazing sheep and collecting honey and firewood, so that for a time they became worse off, even though they were now working harder;

3. that the people became increasingly dissatisfied either with the way their work was organized, or with the basis on which land and crops were allocated, or with both;

4. that work on the project may have upset the customary division of labour between the sexes;

5. that the people resented being 'shown' to so many visitors;

6. that the hard work of planting rice (which the people had never grown before) was the last straw.

The group recognized that the project was a difficult one since it involved many changes in almost every aspect of the people's lives, but it also thought that the extension worker had very little understanding of the human problems involved. This led him to contribute to his own failure:

1. by trying to introduce too many changes too quickly;

2. by not, apparently, consulting the people frequently in order to find out what difficulties they were having in trying to adapt themselves to the requirements of the project;

3. by not leaving them to decide how far and how fast they would go on implementing the project. (The group felt that it was the worker, not the people, who decided how much land should be cleared and where, and what crops should be grown: and that the people were only involved to the extent of doing

E

the work. The group thought that it was this, more than any-thing else, that prevented the worker from realizing that trouble was brewing long before the final breakdown of the project occurred.)

Implications

For this project to succeed—or to have had a better chance of succeeding—the group thought that the extension officer should have tried above all else to get the people to accept the project as *their* project, rather than merely agree to co-operate with him in what, from their point of view, was his project for them. If he had really tried to do this he would have acted very differently, for he would have been mainly concerned to educate, advise, and help them make their own decisions rather than to make decisions for them. Almost certainly the project would then have gone ahead more slowly, but also more surely, for the discussion which would have preceded each decision would have revealed the true attitudes of the people and enabled the worker to deal in time with the difficulties which ultimately caused the project to fail.

As for the worker's comment that the people never showed any initiative in connexion with the project, the group felt that this was because the worker had not given them any real opportunities of exercising it. After all, they showed plenty of initiative later on in relation to their own quite different project of leaving the village and taking their sheep with them!

14. THE CHARTERED BUS

The principal of a training centre encounters trouble when he tries to improve his trainees' holiday arrangements.

THE CASE

Every year since the centre opened seven years ago, all the trainees who could find the small sum of money involved have greatly enjoyed a short camping holiday by the sea.

Because the journey from the training centre to the camp site is a very long one it had always previously been too expensive for them to go by bus. Last year, however, I contracted with a kindly bus-owner that he would do the return trip of 400 miles, plus a reasonable amount of extra mileage at the camp, at about the same cost as going by train. I was delighted, and I thought the trainees would be, too: but as soon as they heard that the trip was to be by bus they demanded to go by train as everyone had always done before.

I explained to them that the camping site was eight miles from the nearest town, and that the bus would be very convenient to get them to and from the site. I warned them of the loneliness of the camping site and of the pleasant evenings they would miss in town if they were without a bus. I also mentioned the two uncomfortable nights they would have to spend on the train. They could not afford to travel by any but the lowest class and they would find the accommodation smelly and dirty.

However, the trainees were adamant. If they couldn't go by train, they said, they wouldn't go at all. In the end, I gave way. I apologized to the bus-owner for cancelling the bus trip and the trainees went by train. They were very sorry afterwards that they hadn't gone by bus.

When this year's trainees asked if they could go to the camp I raised no objection. I said that I would arrange for them to be supplied with food at the camp as I had always done, but that this year they must make all other arrangements, e.g. for transport and launch trips, by themselves. They seemed very unhappy about this, and although they talked about it a good deal afterwards among themselves, this year for the first time there has been no camp at all.

DISCUSSION OF THE CASE

Diagnosis

The members of the group which discussed this case hesitated at first whether to accept it for discussion, some because they did not think it very relevant to problems of community work, and others because they thought it too insignificant to be worth discussing anyway. However, the member who had contributed the case insisted that the problem was a very real one. He had always regarded the camping holiday as an important part of the training course even though it was not officially a part of it, and he had been anxious to make it even better. Yet all he had actually achieved was, first, to create a bad relationship between himself and the trainees who had insisted on going by train; and then to create a situation in the following year when the camping holiday did not take place at all. He would like to get clear why things had gone so badly wrong. He thought it would be useful and hoped that the rest of the group would think so too.

In the end the group agreed to discuss the case, and several ideas were suggested to account for the failure: but the main conclusion, to which everyone agreed, was that the trainees strongly resented the principal deciding to hire the bus without first consulting them. After all, however much authority the principal might quite rightly exercise over the trainees at other times, the camping holiday was a voluntary activity and the trainees paid the transport costs themselves. Therefore they naturally felt that it was for them, not the principal, to decide how their money should be spent: and they strongly resented his assumption that he had the right to decide for them.

If the trainees were as resentful as members of the group thought, this would be quite enough to account for what happened in the case, for the trainees could most obviously assert their right to decide this matter for themselves by refusing to accept the decision to which the principal had already committed himself. But this meant that the trainees felt they simply had to go by train, since even to consider going by bus would seem to condone the very decision they all strongly resented. This, the group felt, was why none of the trainees would agree even to discuss any of the arguments the principal put forward in favour of the bus. At all costs, they were determined to assert themselves by going by train, and it was not till much later, when they were at the camp and their resentment had cooled, that they realized their mistake.

The effect of the bus incident on the principal, the group thought, was to make him determined that he would not lay himself open to any further unhappy experiences of this kind. This was why he told those of the trainees who wanted to go to the camp the following year that although they could go they would have to make all the arrangements themselves. In the event, this proved too much for them to do: partly, perhaps, because they were too inexperienced, since none of them had ever been to the camp before; and partly because, as individual would-be campers, they lacked the skill to organize themselves as an efficient, decision-making group. In effect, therefore, by denying his help the principal also denied them the opportunity of going to the camp.

Implications

If the principal had been aware of the factors highlighted in their diagnosis, members of the group thought, he would not have assumed that he could make the decision. He would have told the trainees about the offer the bus-owner had made and left it with them to decide whether to accept it or not. By acting in this way he would not have aroused their resentment, and they could then have considered the idea much more objectively. In the ensuing discussion of the pros and cons of going by bus or by train he would have had plenty of opportunities of suggesting any points that the trainees did not think of for themselves. The most probable outcome of this discussion, the group felt, would have been a decision to go by bus; but whatever decision was reached the result would have been much better than what actually happened. The good relationship between the principal and his trainees would have been strengthened rather than impaired. He would have provided his trainees with a useful educational experience in decision-making as a group. And he would not have suffered the indignity of having publicly to reverse a decision he had already made.

It was also unfortunate that the principal decided to take no responsibility for making arrangements the following year. This was an understandable reaction on his part but a self-defeating one if he wished the camping holiday to continue, as the course of events showed. What the principal should have done, the group felt, was to encourage the trainees to make the arrangements for themselves while making it clear that he was quite ready to help if and when his help was needed.

15. IMPROVING HOMESTEADS

A small extension team is very successful in getting people to improve their homesteads and replan their farms, but is disappointed when they soon revert to their old ways.

THE CASE

Last year I was in charge of a team working to get the people to improve their homes, replan their farms, and conserve water-supplies by building earth dams.

The team consisted of a community development officer (myself), a community development assistant, an agricultural assistant, a veterinary assistant, and a health assistant. Our idea was to get the people to agree to work together in small voluntary groups. The team would plan the work on each homestead and do enough of it with the help of the group's members to make sure that they knew what they needed to do and how to do it. Then the team would move on to the next homestead and repeat the process until every homestead had been dealt with in the same way. The team would then move on to help another group, leaving the first group to finish the work on their homesteads in their own time.

We were well received when we toured the area to explain what we hoped to do and six volunteers, all neighbours of one another, were quickly forthcoming to form the first group. We made our plans for the first homestead and then quickly got to work. We knocked holes in the walls of the house and put in windows. We plastered and whitewashed the walls inside and out; built an outside kitchen; and made a proper latrine. We also moved all the farm stock into a proper yard where manure could be accumulated for spreading on the land; and we marked out soil conservation terraces. We completed half of these and then moved on to the next house. The six volunteers worked extremely well and went on working after we had left to help another group. It was not long, therefore, before all the work on their homesteads was finished and the result was excellent. The white houses could be seen for miles around.

By this time the scheme had really caught on and we were soon so overwhelmed by requests that five more teams were formed. Dams were built on the same principle, and very soon re-planning and re-building were going on over the whole area.

It was quite a time before the job was finished and the teams disbanded. Everyone agreed that the teams had had a tremendous success. Why then did it happen that the people fell back into their old ways very soon after the teams had left? They started using the bush again instead of latrines; they did not keep up the white-washing and cleansing of their houses; nor did they clean out their dams.

DISCUSSION OF THE CASE

Diagnosis

The members of the group which discussed this case started by seeking to understand why the team had met with such a favourable initial reception. They suggested several factors which might account for this. Thus one reason, they thought, was that the people might have been favourably impressed by some particularly good work previously done by government officers in the area; and another, that the people had heard good reports of community development work done elsewhere and were glad when they heard that work was now to be started in their area also. Some members of the group also thought that the team itself may have made a very good impression. From their reading of the case they thought that the members of the team were probably very keen, very prac-tically minded, and very willing to work with their hands. More-over, their idea of getting the people to form small voluntary groups may well have been very popular if the people of this area, like many rural peoples elsewhere, were already in the habit of working in small groups on each other's farms or for building or repairing each other's houses. If this were so, the team's idea would fit in very well, and it would have the extra attraction that the team was willing to help in doing the work.

The group then went on to discuss why, in spite of the team's favourable reception, it achieved so little of permanent value in the end. The main reason for this, the group felt, was that the members of the team were much too anxious to achieve the greatest possible amount of material change in the shortest possible time. This they succeeded in doing only too well, partly by reason of their genuine success in arousing the enthusiasm of the members of the voluntary groups, and partly because they were so willing to do a great deal of the work themselves.

For the rest, the members of the team appeared to be quite

content that the people trusted them and therefore were willing to work at the various projects they suggested. Apparently they did not even try to educate the people to understand just why all the windows, kitchens, latrines, cattle-yards, terraces and dams were really necessary; or to get them to think out realistically just what other changes, e.g. in habit, custom and daily routine, they would have to accept if they were to make good use of all these innovations. Thus all the team really succeeded in doing was to get the people to complete a series of projects without any real thought for the future and without any real change in their existing outlook, habits and customs. Therefore when the team left, habit reasserted itself, and where this conflicted with the proper use and maintenance of the recent innovations, habit won. This, the members of the group felt, was why the people so quickly reverted to using the bush instead of their new latrines; failed to keep up the whitewashing of their houses; and failed to repair the terraces or clean out the dams.

Implications

The group then went on to think out what the team could have done to avoid this happening. Some members at once suggested that the team should not have got the people working on projects quite so quickly. It would have been much better, they said, to have started by educating them to understand just why and how they would benefit from each of the items included in the team's homestead improvement programme and what they would need to do, and go on doing, in order to reap these benefits after the team had left. They also suggested that the team should have organized a committee of keen and influential local people in each locality to ensure that the people would maintain the homestead improvements when they had completed them.

Some other members of the group, however, felt that such an educational approach would have taken much too long, and that its results would anyway be uncertain. Indeed, they thought that the team might not have been able to get any projects going at all if they had made it clear at the start that the work on the homesteads was only a beginning; and that to get any real benefit from it the people would have to do a great deal more later on as well. On the whole, therefore, they thought that the team's initial approach was a good one, and that its real mistake was in failing to foresee that the people would need supervising afterwards.

Several suggestions were made about how this could have been done. One of them was that the team should have left one of its members behind in each locality in which the team had worked; and another, that the whole team should have revisited every locality every few months to ensure that all the projects were being properly maintained. These were both rejected as impractical since the teams were only temporary and were disbanded when the projects were completed. This led to a suggestion that the needed supervision could have been provided by the ordinary local departmental officers of the district if only the team had sought their co-operation at the outset and planned the scheme with them. Everyone thought that this should have been done, but most members of the group doubted whether even this would have solved the problem completely. Until the people had been educated really to *want*, and hence want to *maintain*, the homestead improvements, they thought, the job of supervising them would be a very heavy one: and far too heavy, in fact, for local departmental officers to undertake in view of all their other commitments, even if they wanted to.

Finally, all the members of the group, albeit some of them rather reluctantly, agreed that the basic approach should have been an educational one. They accepted that this would probably have meant that fewer people would have volunteered to improve their homesteads at the time, but thought that the team would probably have succeeded with some people and that these would have been far more likely to maintain the improvements after the team had gone. As it was, the only lasting result of the team's work—once the people had become disillusioned about their 'improvements' and had let them fall into disrepair—was a situation much less favourable for future development work than the team had itself initially enjoyed.

CONCLUSIONS

The cases studied in this chapter all point to the same two basic conclusions.

1. *While the worker is right to highlight the advantages of the innovation he suggests, he should not try to 'sell' it to the people by stressing only these advantages.*

2. *The worker must try to establish for the innovation a favourable balance of advantage in the light of all the facts, both favourable and unfavourable, from the people's point of view.*

(These are key concepts, but they are often ignored in practice as the cases studied in this chapter show. In all these cases the worker approached his task in much the same way. Having thought of an innovation, he suggested it to the people; explained its advantages as clearly as he could; stated what the people would need to do to obtain these advantages; and what he could do to help. In short, he relied on selling the innovation by stressing its advantages.

In each case the worker seems to have selected an innovation which would have resulted in some real advantage for the people had they accepted it, but in every case he failed because, sooner or later, the people came to realize or suspect that it also entailed some disadvantages for them; and they then rejected the innovation because they felt that *on balance* the disadvantages were greater than the advantage.

Why then did the workers ignore the disadvantages? The reason seems to have been that each of the workers was keen on getting results, and the keener he was the more reluctant he was to investigate the disadvantages of the innovation with the people for fear of endangering its chances of success. But this is bad policy, for if disadvantages exist they will endanger the programme anyway. His best chance of success is to get them openly recognized and expressed. He can then discuss them with the people with a view to finding ways of overcoming or reducing them as was suggested in the discussion of *Helping the Farmers, Conserving the Soil,* and *Turning Nomads into Farmers.* If he succeeds in this, and thus succeeds in establishing a true balance of advantage in favour of the innovation, the people are far more likely to accept it, persist with it, and get real and lasting benefits from it.

It is especially important that the worker should keep to this approach even when the people initially seem quite willing to accept an innovation. As we have seen, the people may sometimes agree merely because they like the worker and are therefore willing to take his ideas on trust, as in *Turning Nomads into Farmers*; or in a sudden but temporary burst of enthusiasm, as in *Improving Homesteads*; or from a mixture of hope and deference to authority, as in *Conserving the Soil*. In fact, the more willing the people initially seem to be, the more need there is for the worker to get them to think out all the pros and cons with care.

By getting the people to investigate both the pros and cons of an innovation instead of merely trying to 'sell' it to them, the worker can greatly increase the likelihood that they will persevere with it once they have made up their minds to accept it. But of course they will not accept it unless they feel that, on balance, its advantages outweigh its disadvantages. It is therefore up to the worker to increase the chances of a favourable outcome partly, as we have already noted, by investigating with the people all practicable ways of reducing some or all of whatever disadvantages there may be; and partly by doing everything possible to ensure that they fully realize all the advantages of the innovation he is suggesting. The importance of identifying and reducing disadvantages is clearly evident from the study of *Helping the Farmers, Conserving the Soil*, and *Turning Nomads into Farmers*. The need to educate people thoroughly to understand the reasons why change is needed is most clearly to be seen in the context of *Conserving the Soil, Turning Nomads into Farmers*, and *Improving Homesteads*. The discussion of the way the soil conservation problem was tackled in *Conserving the Soil* also brings out the point that often the best way of highlighting the need for, and therefore the advantages of, change is to get the people actively involved in investigating facts related to a problem in their own local situation for themselves.

During the process of investigating the balance of advantage the worker and the people educate each other: the worker educating the people about the nature of their problem and ways of solving it; and the people educating the worker to understand their difficulties in putting such ideas into effect. It is then the worker's job to work for a solution which, though not necessarily ideal from the technical point of view, is nevertheless the best solution because it is the best the people are really ready to implement.

The worker who consistently works with people in this way instead of trying to get them to accept his own pre-fixed ideas is much more likely to win the people's trust, and this will stand him in good stead when, as in *The Bee Expert* and *The Cassava Graters*, they are mistrustful of his government's intentions. Had the leader of the team in *The Bee Expert* established such a relationship, for instance, he would have had a real chance of allaying the people's fear of increased taxation if, indeed, they really were unjustified! As it was, not having established such a relationship, he was himself the object of mistrust.

One final point needs to be mentioned. It seems that the students in *The Chartered Bus* did not reject the idea of the bus because they preferred to go by train, or even because they mistrusted the principal's intentions. They rejected it because they resented him deciding for them something they felt they had the right to decide for themselves. In most under-developed areas this is not yet a common cause of failure in community work because so many people have been so accustomed to defer to authority that they tend to accept it without resentment, and sometimes even welcome it. But times are changing, and more and more of these people are now beginning to feel that they have a right to make some decisions for themselves. When people feel like this, the worker needs to be especially careful not to prejudice them against an innovation they might otherwise accept by prejudging whatever it may be they feel they ought to be left free to decide for themselves.)

IMPLICATIONS FOR THE WORKER

Situation: The worker wants to get the people to accept some specific innovation

The workers in the cases included in this chapter have the same basic problem as the workers in the cases included in the previous chapter, but their difficulties are greater for one or more of the following reasons:

1. the people are not aware of the need for the change (Case 12, *Conserving the Soil*);

2. the benefit will come only after a very long time during which they will have to put up with many disadvantages (Case 12, *Conserving the Soil* and Case 13, *Turning Nomads into Farmers*);

3. the innovation will involve change, not at one, but at many points in their existing way of life (Case 13, *Turning Nomads into Farmers* and Case 15, *Improving Homesteads*);

4. they will need to learn new and possibly rather difficult and complex skills (Case 9, *Helping the Farmers* and Case 13, *Turning Nomads into Farmers*);

5. they need to establish some new form of organization, such as a co-operative (Case 11, *The Cassava Graters*).

Suggested Order of Work

A. *Before suggesting the innovation*

1. Define for oneself as clearly as possible the exact need or needs one hopes the innovation will meet.

2. Consider whether the people are already aware of the need. If not, consider in detail what one needs to do in order to make them fully aware of it.

3. Check to make sure that the innovation one intends to suggest is well designed to meet the need that one sees (e.g. that it is technically sound, and also practicable in relation to the local environment, the resources of the people, and the skills they have or can learn).

4. Assess as precisely as one can the balance between the innovation's advantages and disadvantages as the people are

likely to assess them, both while they are considering whether or not to accept it, and afterwards while they are engaged in implementing it.

5. If it seems likely that the people may assess this balance as unfavourable, then consider whether the innovation can be amended so as to reduce the disadvantages.

6. If it cannot be satisfactorily amended, then consider the remaining possibilities (e.g. abandon the attempt; delay it until the balance of advantage becomes more favourable; educate the people in the hope that they will learn to value the advantages of the innovation more than its disadvantages).

7. Consider what skills the people will need to learn in order to adopt the innovation successfully; how many people will need to learn them; how best they can be taught; and who is competent (and available) to teach them.

B. *When suggesting the innovation*

1. First involve the people in discussing and investigating the need, feeding in whatever information may be necessary to help them understand it and assess it. (This information may be given verbally, but preferably also by visual demonstrations either locally or on visits.)

2. *Tentatively* suggest the innovation as a possible means of meeting the need, stressing both the advantages that one anticipates if the people successfully implement it *and* that some disadvantages may also be entailed.

3. Promote discussion with a view to getting the people to assess

    (*a*) the extent of the benefits that the innovation would bring;

    (*b*) whether it would be practicable for them in their local situation and in the light of their existing skills and resources; and

    (*c*) what difficulties and disadvantages they can anticipate.

4. Promote discussion to ascertain to what extent these difficulties and disadvantages could be overcome.

5. Indicate what help, e.g. in teaching any necessary skills or in augmenting scarce resources, one could obtain for them.

6. Suggest any other difficulties or disadvantages, immediate or future, which one fears might endanger the success of the innovation but which the people have so far overlooked.

7. Promote discussion as to how far they are real, and as to how they can be avoided or overcome.

8. Promote discussion with a view to getting the people finally to decide for or against the innovation as amended in the light of the previous discussions.

C. If the people decide in favour

1. Encourage and help them to plan how they will implement the innovation in the light of all the factors previously discussed.

2. Help them to obtain any technical advice they may need.

3. Be sure to keep every promise or undertaking one has made. (See B. 5 above.)

4. Meet the people frequently in order to discuss with them whatever difficulties or problems they may subsequently encounter. (This is very important, for however thorough the preliminary discussions have been it is always possible that some unanticipated problem may arise. If the worker knows about it soon enough, he may be able to help the people to resolve it. If he does not keep closely enough in touch with the people, he may not become aware of it until the people have lost heart and reverted to their former ways as they did in Cases 12, 13 and 14.)

CHAPTER FIVE

Establishing Groups

THE community worker does much of his work with groups either with *representative* groups such as village councils or local community development committees in order to stimulate self help community projects like those discussed in Chapters Two and Three; or with *special interest groups* such as farmers' clubs, women's clubs, self-help housing groups, co-operative groups and the like in order to stimulate group and individual projects.

Such groups provide very favourable situations for community development work. Unlike people in crowds and other *ad hoc* gatherings the members of a group have opportunities of getting to know one another at regular meetings in pursuit of their common purpose, and they nearly always develop some kind of group organization to enable them to achieve that purpose. It is therefore easier in a group than in an *ad hoc* gathering for a worker to get ideas properly considered and discussed: and it is easier for a group, once it has accepted a new idea, to organize whatever collective action may be needed to carry it out.

It is because groups either have or can be helped to develop these characteristics that working with groups is such an important part of community work; and if, as sometimes happens, the worker can find no really suitable group to work with, he may try to get one formed. This is what the worker did in the four cases included in this chapter, but in each case the group soon disintegrated. Study of these cases may therefore highlight some pitfalls that the worker should avoid.

16. THE PARENT–TEACHER ASSOCIATION

The headmaster of a village school starts a parent–teacher association. The parents are enthusiastic at first, but most of them soon cease to attend the meetings.

THE CASE

The Head Teacher of a village school decided that he would like to form a P.T.A. He therefore invited the parents of the pupils to a meeting at the school and asked his local Education Officer to come along too. In the event, forty-five parents came.

The Head Teacher opened the meeting by thanking the parents for coming. He had called the meeting, he said, in the hope that they would agree to establish a P.T.A. He explained that Parent–Teacher Associations already existed in some schools, but that this would be the first in their district. He wanted to start one because he believed that it would lead to teachers and parents working more closely together for the progress and welfare of the children at the school.

Then the Education Officer spoke in support of what the Head Teacher had said. He had had little experience of P.T.A.s himself, he said, but he had heard about the good work they had done elsewhere, and he wanted to congratulate the Head Teacher on wanting to start one. He was sure that the parents would give the Head Teacher their whole-hearted support, and wished them every success in the new venture.

The Head Teacher then invited the parents to ask questions, and when these had been answered he put his proposal to the vote. The parents voted unanimously in favour of it, and a day was fixed for an inaugural meeting to enrol members, appoint a committee, and adopt a constitution. At that meeting the Head Teacher was elected President of the new Association. It was also decided to meet every three months. Everyone was full of enthusiasm.

At the subsequent meetings most of the talking was done by those on the platform. There was little active parent participation except from one or two ill-behaved persons who now and again tried to make trouble, and the Head Teacher was quite able to cope with them. But the parents' early enthusiasm did not last. Attendances dwindled, and after the first few meetings only five or six parents continued to come. The Head Teacher was bitterly disappointed for he had so much wanted to make the Association a success. What went wrong?

DISCUSSION OF THE CASE

Like all the other cases presented in this book, the events described in this case actually happened, but whereas the other cases were contributed by the worker most directly involved, this case was contributed by the Education Officer who had

F

attended only the first meeting. This is why the case gives no specific information about what happened at any of the meetings after the first, and therefore no very specific clues as to why the Association disintegrated. The members of the group which discussed the case would have preferred to study a case which provided more specific information, but none was available which presented this particular kind of problem.

Diagnosis

After considerable discussion the members of the group agreed on the following points, all of which they felt had probably contributed in some way to the failure.

1. The Head Teacher (and the Education Officer!) seemed to have asked the parents to agree to form the Association without themselves thinking out clearly enough beforehand just what purposes they hoped to achieve through the Association, just how they thought they could achieve them, and just what the rights and duties of the members of the Association would need to be. Thus at the meeting the parents agreed to form an Association without any very clear idea of what they were agreeing to: and they agreed because they took what the Head Teacher told them on trust when he said that the Association would result in benefits (unspecified) for their children. When the subsequent meetings of the Association did not result in the kind of benefits the parents wanted, they lost interest and ceased to attend.

2. Members of the group thought that the parents found the meetings unsatisfactory because they had expected to be able to discuss with the teachers many points about the running of the school as it affected them or their children, and with some hope of getting some of these points dealt with. However, they seem to have been given no chance of raising them because the Head Teacher, who was also their President, ran the meeting as he wanted it to be run, and the last thing he wanted was for the parents to raise questions about the way he ran his school. What he wanted was to get the parents to do what *he* wanted for the school. Thus he and the parents were at cross purposes and at the meetings it was his purpose which prevailed.

3. But how then can we account for the parents doing so little to make their feelings known? The group felt that there is evidence in the case that a few parents, the 'ill-behaved' ones, did try, but that they were not supported by the other parents and were ruled out of order by the Head Teacher as President. But in that case, why didn't the other parents support them? The group felt that this could easily be explained. The other parents, they thought, may well have wanted to support them, but did not do so because they were afraid that if they did they would incur the displeasure of the Head Teacher, and that this might prejudice their children's prospects at the school. Hence they remained silent, but lost interest and finally stayed away.

Various other points were suggested which the group thought might also help to explain the failure. Thus some members felt that either the time or the place of the meetings might not have suited the convenience of many of the parents. Others felt that it might have been easier to maintain the parents' interest if the meetings had been more frequent. Others again felt that the Head Teacher might have asked for too much monetary help with the result that the poorer parents (the majority?) may have decided to stay away.

Implications

One implication of their diagnosis, the members of the group felt, was that the Head Teacher should have discussed the objects and functions of the proposed Association with the parents much more thoroughly before it was formed. It was natural that he should want the Association to serve his purpose, but he should have realized that the parents would also have their purposes: that in some respects these purposes might well differ from his own; and that it would be essential, if the Association were to succeed, that the Association should effectively serve both. Thus while *he* might value the Association primarily for the opportunities it would give him of enlisting the help of the parents in solving some of his problems, e.g. of improving the attendance of the children at the school or of providing the school with some needed amenity, *the parents* might value it primarily as a means of influencing him to introduce changes they wanted at the school. Had he recognized this, the members of the group thought, he would have invited the parents to put forward their ideas at the Association's meetings, discussed them with them, and done whatever he could to put them into effect. The parents would then have had a real use for the Association and many more chances of actively participating in its affairs.

The members of the group were divided in their opinion as to whether he should have accepted the office of President, some thinking that he should and some thinking that he could have done better work as an *ex-officio* member of the executive committee. As President, they thought, he would be unduly tempted to use his powers to promote his own purposes at the meetings and to exclude from discussion any topics he did not want discussed. If the points thus excluded were those that some of the parents felt very strongly about, they would then resent the action of the Head Teacher and lose interest in the in the Association, as happened in the case. Thus the Head Teacher had in fact to face up to a dilemma: and whether he could have solved it satisfactorily would depend on several factors: on how objectively he could assess his own purposes and those of the parents; on how competent he was to handle discussion of topics in which his own interests were involved, and on how willing he might be to put his trust in the good sense of the parents and in the genuineness of their desire to help their children at the school.

At this point one of the group's members said he knew of a case of quite unnecessary conflict between a head teacher and an association. The Head Teacher wanted the association to buy a typewriter for use in his office at the school, while the parents thought that a sewing machine was a much more immediate need. It was months before the teacher gave way. Then the sewing machine was brought. The members of the Association used it out of school hours to make uniforms for the children which they sold at a profit, and with the profit thus made they bought the typewriter.

17. THE VILLAGE CO-OPERATIVE

The people respond enthusiastically to the worker's suggestion that they might form a consumers' co-operative. At first
it is very successful but within a year it is dead.

THE CASE

As a community development officer I do a great deal of my work
with village councils and development committees, but I'm always
on the look-out for any other opportunities, however informal, of
getting people to help themselves or the people of the communities
in which they live. Thus when I'm invited to a council or committee
meeting I like to get to the village early so that I can wander round
and talk to people in the streets or in their homes.

In this case I got to Camba village some two hours before the
council meeting was due to start, and as I walked down the street I
noticed a group of six villagers sitting outside a half-built house. I
knew all of them quite well, so I stopped and got into conversation
with them.

After a bit I noticed that we were all smoking and happened to
remark on it, asking how many cigarettes they each smoked in a day.
It seemed that they all smoked at least twenty, and some much more
than that. I then said that it must cost them a good deal and suggested that they might be able to cut down the cost if they formed a
group and each put up a little money in order to buy cigarettes in
bulk. They thought this a wonderful idea. One of them agreed to act
as buyer and seller and they started business with cigarettes and
matches the following day. The six members told others and so the
number increased to ten.

I got them to agree to meet weekly to study the working of consumers' co-operatives and the attendance at these meetings was
quite good. I made a point of taking the first six meetings myself,
and got the co-operative officer to come in too. Meanwhile the business was growing and so was the membership. Good profits were
made. Two more commodities—cooking oil and pitch oil—were
added at the beginning of the second month, and the group added
new commodities at the beginning of each succeeding month. By the
end of the sixth month business had expanded greatly and the
results were very encouraging as far as profits were concerned.

It was soon after this that the monthly takings began to decline,
some members dropping out and others not buying as much as
before. The reason they gave was shortage of cash, but the real

reason, apparently, was the village shop-keeper. The growth of the co-operative had cut his profits and he wasn't too pleased. Of course, he couldn't stop people trading with the co-operative if they wanted to, but he did threaten to stop all credit for every customer who didn't buy every commodity from him, and surprising though it may seem, this was enough. A few months later the co-operative had only two members left.

DISCUSSION OF THE CASE

The members of the group which discussed this case all agreed that it was the shop-keeper's attitude which precipitated the failure, and they all thought that the community development officer should have been aware of this danger from the start. Had he realized it, they said, he would have done much more than he actually did to ensure that the new society was established on a really sound basis, for this might have enabled the society to withstand the shop-keeper's threat.

When they were asked to be more specific, they checked through the case to see just what it was they thought the worker hadn't done, or hadn't done well enough, and queried a number of points. Thus some members thought he was probably wrong to suggest the idea of forming a co-operative himself instead of waiting for the idea to come from the people. Some thought him wrong to start with so few people; others that he should have done more to educate them in co-operative principles after the co-operative had started; others, again, that he should have got the founder members to think things over much more carefully before committing themselves to start: what commodities they would sell, for instance; how much capital they would need; where the store should be sited; what their dividend policy should be; and what arrangements they would need to make to ensure efficient management and effective control by the members. Each of these points was briefly considered and then discarded, for none of them seemed adequate as reasons for the worker's failure in the case. Indeed, most members thought that the worker was right to introduce the idea himself and that it was better to start with a small group, as the worker did, than with a big one. The group also agreed that the worker seemed to have made a real effort to provide an adequate follow-up, and that there was no reason for thinking that the co-operative would have better withstood the effect of the threat the shop-keeper had made if the worker had done anything else.

This brought discussion back to the shop-keeper. Could the community worker have done anything effective about him? One member thought that the worker should have gone to see him right at the start with a view to somehow gaining his support, but everyone else thought this quite impracticable. In a small village, they said, the normal effect of a successful consumers' co-operative must be the ruin of the shop-keeper. This led members of the group to consider whether the worker should have introduced the idea of the co-operative at all, several members maintaining that as a member of the community the shop-keeper had as much right to make a living as anyone else. This was a new idea to some members who had had always assumed that a co-operative was an inherently good thing, and it was only after a good deal of discussion that everyone agreed, some still rather reluctantly, that if the shop-keeper was a good chap and an honest citizen the worker ought to consider his interests just as much as those of anyone else. This forced the group to consider whether the worker had been justified in putting forward his idea of a co-operative at all!

No one felt able to give a definite answer to this question. So much, they thought, would depend on the character of the shop-keeper. If he was a rogue who used this position to fleece the villagers, then they thought the case for a co-operative would be very strong. If on the other hand he provided a good and honest service for no more than a reasonable reward they felt that the case for establishing a co-operative would be very weak if, indeed, there was any case at all.

Implications

What then should the worker actually have done? The members of the group were agreed on only these two points:

1. that he should not have suggested the co-operative without first taking into account the character of the shop-keeper and the effect it was likely to have on his livelihood;

2. that if he then decided to suggest it, he should have been very careful to draw attention to its probable effect on the shop-keeper so that the members of the group would consider whether they really felt justified in putting their own self-interest first; whether, if they did, he had it in his power to make things difficult for them, e.g. by witholding credit; and if so, how they thought they would be able to keep their members loyal.

18. THE TAMARIND TREE GROUP

The worker calls a meeting of the young men of the town to discuss the possibility of forming a young men's association, but none of them come.

THE CASE

Two years ago I was appointed to do community work in a rural district and went to live in the small town (pop. 1,500) which served as its administrative centre. I did most of my work with existing groups but was eager to get new groups established wherever I saw a real need.

One such need I realized almost at once. There was no group for youths to join, and the young men seemed to have nothing better to do than to hang about aimlessly beneath a tamarind tree near the centre of the town. All they ever did was to smoke endless cigarettes and engage in idle talk. If only I could get them and others like them into a group, I thought, I might be able to interest them in some more worth-while activity.

I therefore decided to arrange a meeting and prepared the following notice:

All young men are invited to attend a meeting at 7 o'clock on the evening of Thursday, 21st March at the Public Hall. The purpose of the meeting is to explore the possibility of forming a young men's association.

I took a great deal of trouble to make sure that the meeting was well advertised. I had the notice inserted in the local newspaper; I arranged for it to be read out at every place of religious worship the Sunday before the meeting; and I put up attractive posters to advertise the meeting in different parts of the town. One of the posters I fixed to the tamarind tree itself.

I went to the meeting in good time in order to have a chance of chatting informally with the first arrivals. The hall was empty when I got there but I had expected that. When no one had come by seven o'clock I was a bit disappointed but still not unduly worried, for most people are not very punctual in that town. Then as the minutes passed slowly by and still no one came, my heart sank. I waited and waited until long after I had lost all real hope and then I went sadly home. I'd done my best but clearly my best was not good enough. Why?

DISCUSSION OF THE CASE

Diagnosis

One of the members of the group which discussed this case started the discussion by suggesting that quite probably none of the young men came to the meeting for the quite simple reason that they had not heard about it, but it was soon agreed that this was most unlikely. After all, the community was a very small one and it seemed quite clear that *some* of the young men must have seen the posters (one of which was fixed to the tamarind tree); or read about the meeting in the newspaper; or heard about it from someone who had been to church. If they had been interested they would have told their friends, and some of them would then have attended the meeting.

Thus the group had to look for other reasons and after some further discussion two main ideas emerged: the one, that the young men felt quite satisfied with the way they were already spending their leisure time; and the other, that they suspected and even resented the worker's purpose in suggesting or implying that something more was needed. Each of these two points was then investigated in some detail.

1. *That the young men were quite satisfied with things as they were.*
The members of the group thought that the worker was much too ready to assume that the young men would welcome the idea of forming a new association or group, and that all he needed to do was to suggest it to them. They felt that the young men had in fact already formed their own groups, one of which was the group that met under the tamarind tree, and that as

far as the young men were concerned these groups were suiting their purposes very well. In these groups they were quite free to do what they liked, and what they appeared to like doing was smoking, talking, and enjoying the company of their friends. They were free from all rules and restrictions and could do what they liked as long as they did not interfere with anyone else. The members of the group thought that they probably valued this freedom; wanted to keep it; and suspected that they would lose it if they agreed to merge their group in a larger and more formal association. If they really felt like this it would be quite enough to explain why they kept away from the meeting.

The group thought, however, that some of the young men might have attended the meeting if only the worker had first tried to find out if there was anything that any of the young men would have liked to do, but were unable to do as members of their existing groups. If he had discovered some need of this kind and had advertised the meeting to consider how this need could best be met, the group thought that some of the most interested of the young men *might* have turned up.

2. *That the young men resented the worker's attempt to organize them*

The group felt that this was also a major factor. Since the notice sent out by the worker gave no clear indication of what needs the proposed association was intended to meet, the young men were left to conjecture these for themselves; and their most likely conclusion, members of the group felt, would be that its real purpose was to provide a means of bringing them much more closely under adult supervision and control. They would dislike the idea of this, and they would also resent the implication that they were in need of supervision and control. They would do their best to avoid it, and the simplest way of doing so was to boycott the meeting. (Incidentally, it is worth remarking at this point that the members of the group thought that the young men would have been quite right in suspecting that the worker was trying to 'capture' them for his own purposes. In their view the worker provided a good deal of evidence of this in his statement of the case. Thus he refers to the way they spent their time 'aimlessly'; to their smoking of 'endless cigarettes'; and to 'the idle talk' they engaged in. All this, they thought, clearly indicated what the worker's attitude to the young men was.

Implications

When the members of the group began to discuss the implications of their diagnosis, a few of them felt that the worker should have recognized that the young men were already meeting their own needs for themselves, and that all he needed to do was to leave them alone. Most of the group, however, felt that the worker was right in trying to do something: both for the sake of the young men whom some thought would enjoy doing something more active if only they knew what to do; and for the sake of the community which might suffer if boredom led the young men into mischief and anti-social activities. But although most members of the group were agreed that the worker therefore ought to do something, at first they were very unclear about just what it was he should have done. It was only after much discussion that the following points were agreed on:

1. the worker should not have attempted to call a meeting until he was sure that some at any rate of the young men would be interested in establishing some new kind of group;

2. in order to be sure of this he needed to meet and make friends with some of the young men, and get them to introduce him to the other members on their group;

(The members of the group discussing the case all thought that the worker should start by contacting individual young men. They thought that he should not make a direct approach to any group until he had made friends with at least one or two of its members.)

3. on the basis of the friendly relationship thus established tactfully to find out what interests any of the young men might have which they could not pursue in their existing groups;

4. in relation to any such interests in any group, or among some of the members of several groups, to consider what he

could best do to help any one or more of the existing groups to get what they seemed to want (e.g. coaching for football, a place to play games, or a place to dance); or, if only a few members from each of several groups were interested, he might then consider proposing the formation of a new club in which they could pursue it together (e.g. a football club, a games club, or whatever it might be);

(It was suggested at this point that the worker might usefully have approached the local employers of the young men (a) to find out more about their characters and leadership qualities, and (b) to get the employers interested in providing some material help. The members of the group thought that an approach for the second purpose might be very useful if the worker lacked resources of his own, but they felt that the worker would be most unwise to ask employers for their personal opinions about individual young men. Such opinions would often be so biased or so irrelevant to the worker's purpose that they would not be worth having. Moreover, there was always the risk that the young men would hear that the worker had been inquiring about them and this could only serve to intensify any existing feelings of suspicion or mistrust.)

5. then, and only then, when he knew some of the young men were interested, to call a meeting to discuss the details of establishing any proposed new group.

To sum up, the members of the group felt that although the worker was right in trying to do something, he set about his task in quite the wrong way. They thought this was because he failed to recognize that he had neither the right, nor the power, to get the young men to conform to his own pre-fixed ideas of what was good for them. What he did have was a duty to investigate their needs and interests and try to meet them as acceptably as he could. The members of the group thought that this was a very difficult thing to do and that if the worker had realized this he would have proceeded very carefully. His key problem, they thought, was to get some of the young men to accept him as their friend, and he should have been prepared to bide his time, possibly for several months, until a favourable opportunity presented itself of getting to know one or two of them, e.g. a chance meeting at a young man's home while visiting his parents for some quite different purpose.

19. THE GROCERY STORE

The worker unsuccessfully tries to establish a consumers' co-operative after two earlier attempts had failed.

THE CASE

Some years ago I was posted to a district in which there were several large commercially-owned plantations, each of which employed a large number of workers. Most of these workers lived in villages close by the plantations which employed them.

I got on particularly well with the people of one village, won their confidence, and succeeded in establishing several groups of different kinds. One of these groups was a credit union. It did very well, and it was this success that gave me the idea of trying to establish a consumers' co-operative also.

There was a real need for a group of this kind in that village, and both the villagers and the management of the plantation were already aware of it. In fact, the management had already tried twice to set up some kind of co-operative grocery store, but had failed both times. On the first occasion, the management decided which of the workers should be responsible for running the store, but they were so ignorant, careless, and even dishonest, that they soon ran up a debt of £400 and the store had to be closed. On the second occasion the management arranged for its plantation accountant to supervise the group's finances and for a time all went well. The original debt of £400 was paid off, the group flourished, and finally the plantation management decided that the time had come to allow the group to carry on without its accountant's supervision. That was the start of fresh trouble. The group again became insolvent and the store was closed for a second time.

However, the success of the credit union gave me real confidence that I could succeed where the plantation's management had failed, so I talked about my idea to some of the leading people in the village. They did not seem very keen, but they agreed to call a village meeting to discuss it.

I tried very hard to ensure the success of this meeting. Not only did I give a talk myself, but I also arranged for a co-operative officer to show them a film, give them a talk, and help me to answer the people's questions afterwards. But we got nowhere. Everyone agreed that they badly needed a consumers' co-operative, but no one was willing to join one, or help to run it or lend money to it, because they were so sure it would fail. Thus when I asked if the credit union would lend money for the project, its members wanted to know who would repay the thefts this time.

So nothing was done and the need remains unmet. Could I have acted more successfully?

DISCUSSION OF THE CASE

The members of the group which discussed this case thought that in trying to get a consumers' co-operative started in this village the worker set himself an exceptionally difficult task: partly because a consumers' co-operative is a particularly difficult kind of group to get successfully established anyway; but more especially in this case because of the two unsuccessful experiences which the people of this community had already had. These had obviously made the people in this village realize very clearly just how great the risks and dangers inherent in the management of a consumers' co-operative were. Thus, although they would have been happy to enjoy the benefits of the cheaper goods or dividends that it could bring, they were quite unwilling to take risks this would involve. In particular, no one was willing to risk his own money by taking shares in the proposed new venture or by lending money to it.

The members of the group also thought that the success of the credit union had probably had an effect quite different from what the worker had expected. The credit union would have been a relatively small group of the more intelligent and forward-looking people in the village, who all had every reason to take an active interest in the affairs of their union since it was their own money which was at stake. The effect of this would have been to make them more wary rather than more eager to involve themselves financially in a consumers' co-operative which would have a much larger membership—the affairs of which would be more difficult to control. All their experience in the credit union would encourage them to regard the consumers' co-operative as a bad risk, and the worker would have to be able somehow to convince them that their money would be completely safe before they would agree to lend money to it.

Implications

The members of the group felt that the worker had neglected to take these several factors sufficiently into account. Had he done so, they thought, he would have made a much more cautious approach and would not have called a village meeting until a great deal of background thinking and planning had been done. For this, he should have collected a small group of the most responsible and intelligent of the village people, including the leaders of the successful credit union, and suggested that if they still thought that a consumer's co-operative would be useful they might consider investigating in detail the reasons for the difficulties which had caused previous failures, with a view to seeing whether they could be effectively overcome. Had he done this, he might have got the members of the group to consider quite specifically and concretely just what was needed to safeguard any new attempt from the mistakes that had caused them to fail in the past. Each need could then have been considered and ways of meeting it discussed. Thus one obvious need was a trained accountant—at least for some time to come. Would the plantation management still be willing to help, or could one be got from any other source? Could one be got who would be willing to train as well as supervise? What other checks would be needed? How could they most effectively be provided and who, if anyone, could really be relied on efficiently to carry them out? If no really satisfactory answer could be found to each of the specific points, then indeed the worker and the members of the group would have convinced themselves that the project had no hope of success: but to the extent that satisfactory answers were found, so the confidence of the members would grow and their attitude change. Only when, and if, the members of the group had satisfied themselves that they could start up the new co-operative with a really good chance of success, and were willing to try, should the worker have got them to call a village meeting. At this meeting the worker and the co-operative officer should have been present, but they should have kept themselves in the background unless specifically asked to speak. In the main the task of convincing the villagers that the new proposals were sound, and would work, should be left to the group of leading villagers whom the worker had encouraged and helped to think them out.

CONCLUSIONS

1. *People will not agree to form a group unless they believe that it will meet some need or serve some purpose of their own.*

(A worker who decides to try to form a group has by implication already made a provisional judgement about three things:
- (*a*) that a need exists for such a group;
- (*b*) that people are already aware of, or can be made aware of, some need the group can help to meet; and
- (*c*) that people will agree with the worker that the need can best be met by forming such a group.

If the worker's judgement is sound on all these points he has a good chance of establishing a successful group, but if he is wrong about any one of them then he is likely to fail. This is well illustrated by the course of events in Case 18, *The Tamarind Tree Group.* In that case the young men had already formed groups to meet the needs they saw. They were unaware of needing the kind (what kind?) of 'worth-while activities' the worker wanted to provide. Hence they proved quite unwilling to join the kind of group the worker wished to form. This suggests that before trying to form a group the worker should first carefully check just what need the proposed new group will meet; whether this is a need the people already feel; and whether it is already met, or can be met, by some existing group or groups.)

2. *People will not continue to support a group unless it meets, and goes on meeting, some need or purpose of their own.*

(It may be relatively easy to start a group, but it is easier still for it to fail. This is because when people join a group they expect it to meet some need or serve some purpose of their own. While it does this they will support it and the group will flourish. When it ceases to do so they will quickly lose interest and withdraw their support—and the group will then begin to break up.

In Case 16, *The Parent–Teacher Association*, the head teacher succeeded in forming a group in the first instance because the people thought that his purpose and theirs were the same. When after a time they realized that he was using the group only for his purpose, and that this was different from their own, they acted as the young people had done in the case of *The Tamarind Tree Group* and simply stayed away. This suggests that the worker must always ensure that whatever his own particular purpose with the group may be, the group will also adequately meet the needs and serve the purposes of its members.)

3. *When forming a group the worker needs to be able to anticipate whatever major difficulties the group may subsequently have to face and also how its members can be helped to avoid or overcome them.*

(For the members of a group to achieve their purposes they need some knowledge, skill and resources, and to the extent that they cannot provide all they need for themselves they will need help from outside. When a worker takes it upon himself to start a group, he must also be able to see his way to providing whatever outside help may be needed.

The worker in Case 17, *The Village Co-operative*, was aware of this and tried to provide what was needed by arranging for the members to meet weekly to learn how a consumers' co-operative should be run. This was excellent as far as it went, but it did not go far enough. The members also needed to be reminded to take into account the likely reactions of others—in this case the shop-keeper—to the activities of the group: and had the worker done this at the start the people (and the worker!) might have decided not to form the group at all. To leave even one major difficulty overlooked, and hence not provided against, is to risk an unnecessary failure.

G

One bad effect of failure is that it tends to weaken the people's confidence in their own ability to help themselves: and the main problem of the worker in Case 19, *The Grocery Store*, was how to get the people to face up to difficulties which had already defeated them twice, and of which they were therefore only too well aware. Whatever he did he could not be sure of succeeding, but study of the case suggests that his best approach under the circumstances would have been to help the people or their leaders to think out in specific detail just what they could do to safeguard themselves in the future from the weaknesses and shortcomings that had caused them to fail in the past. To the extent that he succeeded, so he would be rebuilding their confidence to the point where they might become willing to try again.)

IMPLICATIONS FOR THE WORKER

Situation: The worker sees a need which he thinks can best be met by forming a new group

Suggested Order of Work

A. *Before suggesting that a group should be formed*

1. Define as clearly and specifically as possible just what need (or needs) one thinks the proposed new group will help to meet.

2. Consider whether the people one hopes will join are already aware of such a need. If not, consider how one can try to make them aware of it.

3. If they are already aware of it, check whether they are already meeting it through membership of any existing groups.

4. If the need exists and is not satisfactorily being met, consider whether when the group is formed its members are likely to have among themselves whatever knowledge, skills and resources they will need to achieve their purposes for the group.

5. If their resources seem inadequate, consider how they can be supplemented from outside the group.

6. List every source of difficulty the members are likely to encounter when they have formed the group, and

consider what steps one needs to take to ensure that as far as possible the group will be able to deal effectively with them.

7. Decide whether to try to establish the group or not.

B. *When suggesting the group*

1. Pre-test one's ideas with some of the local people, both community leaders and people of the kind one hopes will join.

2. Get some of them to call a public meeting to discuss the forming of the group.

3. At the meeting and as opportunity offers

> (*a*) get the people to consider whether a need for such a group exists, and if so just what purposes they have that it could serve;
>
> (*b*) get them to decide how the group should be established, and managed once it has been formed;
>
> (*c*) promote discussion leading to some general agreement about what its programme of activities should be;
>
> (*d*) draw attention to the kinds of difficulties the group might encounter in doing what it is suggested it should do;
>
> (*e*) get these difficulties discussed with a view to seeing how they can be overcome;
>
> (*f*) indicate what kinds of help oneself or one's agency can provide.

C. *If the people decide in favour of forming the group*

Ensure that any help one has promised is provided as and when needed. (See B. 3(*f*) above.)

CHAPTER SIX

Working with Groups

THE purposes of a community worker are never quite the same as those of the members of the groups with which he works. The purposes of the members are related to the needs and interests that led them to join the group. The purposes of the worker are those he hopes to achieve through contact with the members of the group. These purposes may be quite *specific* as when he has some project or activity he hopes to influence them to undertake; or they may be *general* in terms of helping them to get on better with one another, agree on what it is they want to do, learn what is needed to put their decisions into effect, and feel responsible for the welfare of each other and of people outside the group.

The worker has to try to achieve such purposes through what he says and does when he meets the group's members. Some of these contacts may be with individual members, but he is likely to do most of his work while attending meetings of the group. Each of the cases included in this chapter shows the worker actually at work in a group meeting and in each case he runs into some difficulty that he lacks the skill to overcome. Study of these cases, therefore, may help to throw light on some of the problems that workers with groups have to face. It may also lead to some conclusions about how such problems can best be more effectively dealt with.

20. THE COMMUNITY PROJECT THAT WASN'T

A first community project is successfully completed, but a second project fails because of what happened during discussion of the first.

THE CASE

I am a community development worker, and it is my job to get rural people interested in undertaking self-help projects to improve their communities. I've had a good many successes, but also some failures. It is one of these failures that I want to tell you about now.

The whole thing started when the District Health Officer asked me one day if I thought I could get the people of the village of Aurora to put in a pipe to supply pure water to their school. The school's existing supply was very dirty and had to be brought to the school from a long way off.

Well, I put the idea to the village development committee. They received it favourably on the whole, but some of them wanted the water brought right into the centre of the village so that everyone could have it. Unfortunately, however, the spring from which the water was to be piped was very small and could not possibly provide enough water for everyone. When I told them this, one of the committee members, a Mrs. de Souza, said straight out that if the spring was too small to supply the whole village she saw no point in discussing the idea any further. She thought it would be much better to find some other project that would suit everyone.

This was too much for the schoolmaster, Mr. Lawson, who hastened to defend the scheme. He pointed out that the school was a long way away from the village well, and he stressed his difficulties at the school where water was always running short, and most of all in the hot weather. 'It's a real nuisance at times,' he said, 'and I for one think we have enough public spirit in this community to get support for this project. Besides, it needn't be only for the school. If the project goes through I shall be quite willing to let people get water there after school hours.'

This helped to veer opinion in favour of the project, and when at last the Chairman suggested that the committee should declare in favour of it, even Mrs. de Souza grudgingly agreed. I went home that night feeling that I had done a good day's work, and within the next three months the pipe was laid.

A bit later on I went back to Aurora to see if I could get another project started. This time I had no particular scheme in mind. Thus when I had met the committee and congratulated its members on the good work they had already done, I merely asked if they were thinking of tackling another project, and if so was there anything I could do to help.

Several members of the committee at once said that they had been thinking about building a village hall and were wondering whether I would be able to help them get a grant. They wanted a hall badly as they had nowhere to meet except the school, and that was not always convenient. I promised to do my best to get them a grant and said that I could also help with the plans. I then inquired about the site and was told by the schoolmaster, Mr. Lawson, that he and the Chairman had found a good site near the school, and that the owner was willing to give it free.

That seemed hopeful enough. We then got down to discussing details of planning and in due course I was able to get them a grant. Thanks to the energy of the Chairman, the schoolmaster, and most other members of the committee, the people accepted the project, cleared the site, and put in the foundations. But all was not really well. Apparently, Mrs. de Souza had neither forgotten nor forgiven her defeat over the previous project. She harboured a grudge against the schoolmaster, and was further embittered because this second project was also near the school. She lived at the far end of the village and benefited least of all. She hadn't felt strong enough to challenge the committee openly, but now she did everything in her power to stir up discontent among her friends. What was even worse, she got up a petition which she sent to the Minister.

I knew nothing of all this until one day I found a letter on my desk from the head of my department. It read as follows:

'I have to inform you that our Minister has been sent a Petition signed by 97 of the residents of Aurora protesting that the site selected for their new Village Hall is too far from the centre of the village, and complaining that they were not properly consulted at the time it was chosen.

'You must be aware that I have issued strict orders that officers must not encourage any village project unless they have satisfied themselves that it is supported by everyone concerned. I am therefore at a loss to understand the situation that has now arisen. Until this matter has been investigated you are in no way to commit this Department to any further action in connexion with it.'

Well, that was that. Having that Mrs. de Souza on the committee was a piece of bad luck. She's stirred up real trouble in that village and I don't think there's much chance of that village hall getting finished for a long time to come. But what can you do when you come up against people like that? What would you have done?

DISCUSSION OF THE CASE

Some members of the group which discussed this case at first did not think that it presented a suitable problem for discussion. They put all the blame on Mrs. de Souza and thought the worker very unlucky to have had a woman like that on the committee. She was a born trouble-maker. That was all there was to it, and there was no point in discussing the case any further.

Others disagreed. They maintained that it is the job of the community worker to work with people as he finds them, and that there are many people like Mrs. de Souza sitting as members of village committees. They agreed that such people are very difficult to work with, but felt that workers must learn how to cope with the difficulties they present. They regarded this as an essential skill, without which the worker was likely often to do a great deal of harm. In the present case for instance, they thought that the main effect of the worker's work, apart from the one completed project, was to turn what initially appeared to be a reasonably united community into a community divided between two factions— the one headed by the schoolmaster and the other by Mrs. de Souza—quarrelling over a half-finished project and with bad feeling everywhere. This was a direct result of the worker's work, and in their view the harm he had done had far outweighed the good.

Diagnosis

The group then accepted the case for study and started by trying to understand why Mrs. de Souza had acted as she did. They found nothing in the case to suggest that she came to the first meeting of the village committee intending to cause trouble. On the contrary, she seemed very keen. Her only fault, if it *was* a fault, was that she was not very keen on the project the worker wanted because she wanted the piped water for the *whole* village. And all she did when the worker said that this could not be done was to say quite reasonably that she thought they ought to reject the worker's suggestion in favour of some other project 'that would suit everyone'. This was a perfectly reasonable reaction, and none of the members of the group could find any evidence to suggest that she was anything but keen and co-operative up to this point.

What changed Mrs. de Souza's attitude for the worse seems to have been the speech by the schoolmaster. By saying that he was sure 'we have enough public spirit in this community to get support for this project' he implied that Mrs. de Souza was lacking in public spirit, and the group thought that Mrs. de Souza must have felt that this remark was quite unnecessarily insulting, coming as it did just after she had spoken against accepting the project. They also thought that she resented it all the more keenly since it was the schoolmaster himself who most clearly had everything to gain by getting the project accepted. Nor would she feel any less resentful when the schoolmaster went on to appeal to the self-interest of some of the committee members by promising to allow people who lived near the school to get water there after school hours. Mrs. de Souza lived at the far end of the village and would benefit least of all.

The members of the group now understood and sympathized with her feelings. They also noted that she did not express them at the time. In fact she did nothing to cause trouble until, as she saw it, the schoolmaster managed to get the *second* project sited to suit himself near the school. It was this, the group thought, that so intensified her resentment against the schoolmaster that it drove her to the course of action described in the case.

Feeling that they could now understand why Mrs. de Souza had acted as she did, and incidentally feeling much more sympathy for her than they had at the start, the members of the group went on to consider how far they thought the worker was responsible for the way things had turned out. They concluded that he was in fact responsible on two counts: the one, that he did something he ought not to have done or should have done differently; and the other, that he omitted to do something that he should have done.

What he did was to suggest a specific project which benefited some members of the committee (the schoolmaster and those who lived nearest to the school) much more than those who (like Mrs. de Souza) lived farthest away from it. It was this that introduced the seed of conflict. What he did not do, since he wanted the project to go through, was to realize that Mrs. de Souza's initial reaction was quite a natural and reasonable one and therefore help her to get her objection properly discussed. On the contrary, he was very happy to sit back and watch the schoolmaster attack Mrs. de Souza and push the project through. It was this that caused the seed of conflict to grow.

Implications

Although members of the group reached an agreed diagnosis, they found it much more difficult to agree about its implications for the worker. Thus some members felt very strongly that a worker should never try to get a community to accept any pre-fixed idea of his own, and that the worker in the case ran into trouble simply because he neglected this basic principle. In their view he should have gone to the committee solely in order to find out what project, if any, its members could all agree on. The members of the committee might have suggested several projects from which they would ultimately have chosen the one project that suited them best. The idea of supplying piped water to the school would probably not have occurred to them: but if the schoolmaster had suggested it it would then have been only one of several ideas put forward by the committee members, all of which would have been considered on their merits. If the worker had approached the committee in this way, and if he had been solely interested in helping the members to choose a project on which they could *all* agree, Mrs. de Souza would have had a much better chance of getting her own ideas properly considered: and she would then have had much less cause to harbour resentment whatever project had been finally agreed on.

Other members of the group, however, felt that this was all very well in theory but all too often unrealistic in practice. This was so, they said, because a worker was not always able, even if he wanted to, to leave the people quite free to choose their own project for themselves. Quite often the worker might have to try to get them to accept some specific project that his agency would like. If this was the situation of the worker in the case under discussion, and some members of the group thought it was, it was no good saying to him that he should not have suggested the project at all. For him the real problem was how to get the project accepted without offending Mrs. de Souza.

Everyone agreed that workers whose freedom was restricted in this way had many extra difficulties to overcome and sometimes a quite impossible job to do: but having said this, they decided to try to see how, if at all, the worker might have succeeded in this case. They discussed this problem at length, and various ideas were suggested and role-played, but none seemed to offer any real chance of success. The most hopeful approach, assuming that the worker suggested the project himself and that both Mrs. de Souza and the schoolmaster reacted to it as they had done in the case, seemed to be that the worker should intervene *in support of Mrs. de Souza* after the schoolmaster's first speech: his purpose in doing so being to affirm his belief in her good intentions and her right, equally with all other members of the committee, to state her views and have them thoroughly considered and discussed. If the worker had recognized Mrs. de Souza in this way, the members of the group thought, whatever the outcome Mrs. de Souza's resentment would have been much less, if, indeed, she remained resentful at all. If the worker had done this, however, it would have weakened his chances of getting his project through.

Whatever he had done at this first meeting the members of the group felt that the worker made things worse by what he did, or rather did not do, at the meeting at which the second project was discussed. It was true that at this meeting the worker suggested no project of his own, but the group thought that he was much too ready to assume that the village hall project put forward by some of the committee members was acceptable to them all. They felt that he should have asked if this were really so, or whether any of the members had any other ideas they would like to have discussed. Similarly, when the schoolmaster said that he and the Chairman had found a site, he should have asked if everyone agreed that the site was a really suitable one. Had he done this he would have provided other members with a chance to make their views known. Indeed, the group thought that in both meetings the worker was far too ready to assume that the silence of the silent member meant consent, whereas in fact with some at least it hid strong inner feelings of resentment.

21. HE MEANT WELL

A community development worker tries to help the members of a newly-formed village development committee to learn how to conduct their meetings more efficiently, but finds that his efforts are not appreciated.

THE CASE

Some years ago I was appointed to a certain district to work with village development committees in relation to whatever projects they might wish to undertake. I got on quite well until one day I ran into difficulties at a meeting of a newly-formed committee, and it is this I want to tell you about now.

The Chairman and committee members greeted me very warmly, and I was feeling very happy when we got down to business. However, this feeling did not last for I soon realized that I was in for a really bad meeting. The members of the committee were keen enough but none of them had any idea about how a meeting should be run and their Chairman, Mr. Wong, least of all. He did nothing to keep the members in order, and since most of them were pushing their own pet schemes and arguing against the schemes of others, you can imagine what it was like. There was hardly a moment when three or four people were not talking at once.

I stuck it as long as I could but then I felt I could bear it no longer. Luckily, I was sitting next to the Chairman, so I pointed out what was happening and suggested that they would get on much better if he called the members to order and asked them to address their remarks to him instead of arguing among themselves as most of them were doing.

Well, I suppose he did his best, but his best was not much good. He rapped on the table and told them what I had said, but within a minute or two things were just as bad as before. Of course, the real

59290

trouble was that he had no idea at all of how to chair a meeting, and in a meeting like that it was quite impossible to try to teach him. Meanwhile, time was getting on. I realized that I would soon have to go, but I wanted to do something, and it seemed to me that the best thing to do would be to offer to come out again for their next meeting to show them how a meeting ought to be run.

So that is what I did. I put my suggestion as tactfully as I could. Everyone seemed to think that it was quite a good idea. They agreed to meet again in two weeks' time, and I came away quite happy. It was true that the meeting had been a very bad one and that it had ended without any project being decided on, but I felt that there was now a real chance that things would go better next time.

However, a few days later I received the following letter:

'Thank you very much for so kindly visiting our committee meeting. It was good of you to come since we all know how busy you are. Regarding our next meeting, we have talked it over and feel it would be better if you did not come until after we have had a few more meetings and got more experience, as we do not want to waste too much of your time. Of course we shall be very pleased to see you later on.'

It was a polite letter, but its meaning was clear enough. Rather than have me back they would prefer to muddle through on their own. But why? After all, all I had done was to try to help them?

DISCUSSION OF THE CASE

(This case was contributed in 1956 and was produced as a sound film strip by the group which first discussed it. It has been discussed by many subsequent groups, all of which have diagnosed it in much the same way and drawn similar conclusions from it. Although the outline of discussion which follows is based primarily on the course of discussion in *one* group, one or two additional points have been introduced from discussions in other groups.)

The members of the group which discussed this case started by assessing the extent of the worker's failure. They did this by comparing the situation at the beginning of the case with that at the end. What had the worker in fact achieved? The members of the committee were obviously keen. It was the worker's job to help them agree on a project and plan how they would do the work. This he had certainly failed to do. But he had done something and this, in the opinion of the members of the group, was to worsen his own position *vis-à-vis* the committee. The members of the committee started by valuing his presence with them. They ended by not wanting him back for their next meeting. Thus as well as failing to help them at the meeting he attended, he had also destroyed whatever chance he might have had of helping them at future meetings.

The members of the group then went on to discuss why the committee did not want him back. They concluded that there were two main reasons for this: the one, that he had not provided any of the help they expected him to provide; and the other, that he had antagonized them by the tactless nature of what he did.

What he did was to intervene twice. On the first occasion he spoke directly to the Chairman criticising the behaviour of the committee's members (and by implication the behaviour of the Chairman too!) and telling him what he ought to do. This, the members of the group thought, was quite the worst thing the worker could have done. It did not really help the Chairman since he seems to have lacked the skill to put the worker's advice into effect. All it did was to make him aware that the worker was dissatisfied with the meeting and blaming him for it. Members of the group also thought that neither the Chairman nor the committee members particularly valued the worker's opinion about how the meeting should be run. What they were interested in was choosing what project they wished to undertake.

In the opinion of the members of the group, the worker's second intervention was even more disastrous than the first. By offering to come back 'to show them how a meeting ought to be run' he repeated and re-emphasized all the mistakes he had made when he had intervened before. However tactfully he tried to say it, it must have been abundantly clear to the Chairman and committee members that he thought them quite incompetent to conduct their own meetings by themselves: and however true this may have been—and possibly just because it was so true—they would naturally resent this being pointed out to them by a comparative stranger. The group also thought that he made things even worse by getting up to leave before the meeting was over; and worse again by suggesting to the committee that they should accept *his* purpose (that they should learn committee procedure) for their next meeting, at the expense of continuing with *their* purpose which was to discuss which project they should choose. The members of the group thought that the committee only agreed to this to avoid further embarrassment while the worker was present, and that the letter was devised as the politest way of telling him that they did not want him any more.

Implications

When the members of the group had completed their diagnosis they were clearer about what the worker should not have done than about what he ought to have done. All they were initially agreed on was that he had somehow to intervene; that he had to do it without incurring the resentment either of the Chairman or of the committee's members; and that he needed to get on with his real job of helping the committee agree on what project it wished to undertake. The members of the group all felt that this presented the worker with a difficult problem and they discussed it at length, putting up many ideas and role-playing some of them, until they finally agreed on the following conclusions:

1. The worker should preferably have got to the meeting at least half an hour before it was due to start.

(The members of the group thought this particularly desirable in this case as the committee was a newly-formed one and the worker was meeting its members for the first time. They thought it important that he should have a chance of chatting with the members informally and establishing a friendly relationship with them and especially with the Chairman before the meeting started. This, they thought, would be helpful when the time came for him to intervene during the meeting.

2. He should have asked the Chairman to allow him a few

minutes at the beginning of the meeting to explain who he was
and what he could do to help the committee with whatever
project it might decide to undertake,

(Some members of the group thought that some at least of
the members of the committee might not know just what the
worker could do to help them, e.g. by forwarding their application for a grant, by getting them technical advice, and by
helping them with any difficulties they might meet. They
thought it important that they should know this as this, too,
might help the worker when he wanted to intervene.)

3. When he decided that the time had come to intervene
he should

> (a) start by congratulating the members of the com-
> mittee on their keenness and on the variety of ideas
> they were putting forward;
>
> (b) say that he was most anxious to hear each of the
> ideas thoroughly discussed by everyone, so that he
> could clearly understand all the various issues
> involved;
>
> (c) suggest to the Chairman that he might think it a
> good idea to list all the projects the members were
> suggesting so that the whole committee could
> thoroughly discuss each of them in turn;
>
> (d) suggest that if in the end they found it difficult
> to agree on any one of the projects, they might
> consider choosing two or even three. In that case
> their main job would be to decide on the order of
> priority of the various projects, and on this they
> might find it easier to agree.

The members of the group felt that the committee would
have welcomed the worker intervening in this way, which
was in no way critical of the members. They would have felt
happy that the worker recognized their keenness, and compli-
mented by his request to hear all their ideas for projects
thoroughly discussed. The Chairman would probably have
welcomed the idea of making a list, which he would have been

quite able to do and which would have made his job of controlling the meeting much easier. The members of the group also thought that if the worker had thought of suggesting that the committee might choose several projects and list them in order of priority, this would have made the Chairman's job easier still by reducing the intensity of the conflicting interests represented on the committee.

Had the worker acted in this way, they felt, the chances were that the members of the committee would have agreed on a project (or several projects) by the end of the meeting, and felt correspondingly pleased both with themselves and with the worker. Incidentally, he would also have helped them to understand some of the elements of committee procedure—at least as far as the importance of keeping to an agenda was concerned.

22. THE NURSERY SCHOOL

A Head Teacher finds it difficult to reconcile her position as an employee of a government education department with her responsibilities as president of her local Parent–Teacher Association.

THE CASE

I have been in charge of the kindergarten department of my school for many years, and all the parents know that I have the interests of their children very much at heart. That is why, I suppose, they did me the honour of electing me president of their Parent–Teacher Association some time ago. I was delighted, of course, and very eager to help them in any way I could.

In our community the mothers of even young children have to go out to work. This was why at the very first meeting after my election many of the parents spoke out very strongly about their need for a nursery school, and a motion was passed instructing the executive committee to see what could be done.

When the committee met to discuss the problem, everyone felt that it was up to the government to provide the school. After all, the ruling party had come out in favour of such schools at the last election, and now was the time for them to do something about one

Some members of the committee, however, did not rate our chances very high. As one of them said, 'You all know as well as I do what government departments are like. They never do anything unless they have to. What we've got to do is to find some way of bringing real pressure to bear.'

It was then that I had an idea. The Chief Inspector of Primary Schools had already promised to come to our Speech Day which was due shortly, so I suggested that I might make a point of referring to our need for a nursery school in my speech, and that we should get the parents to applaud each point I made as loudly as they could. If they demonstrated loudly enough this would help to bring home to the Inspector how very strongly they felt about it. The committee thought this a very good idea and one of the members said he would tip off the press to make sure that the newspapermen would be present.

Well, that Speech Day surely was something. It was reported in all the papers the next day and the Chief Inspector was certainly impressed and even a bit embarrassed. He couldn't promise anything at the meeting, of course, but he asked me to send in a full statement of why the nursery school was needed and said that he would do his best to see if something could be done.

This raised our hopes, naturally, but we had to wait a long time for a reply, and then it only came after several reminders. And when it did come, it was most disappointing. Our Head of Department either would not or could not do anything. The excuse he gave was that all available funds for a long time to come were to be spent on expanding secondary education, and that he had no funds at all for building or maintaining nursery schools.

When I read this letter to the members of my executive committee they were very angry and accused the government of bad faith. Nor were they willing to let the matter rest there. What they now wanted to do was to get up a petition and appoint a delegation to take it to the Minister. As one of them said, 'We'll show that damned civil servant, your Head of Department, where he gets off!'

And that's the position at this moment. I managed to get them to agree to wait till after the next full meeting of the P.T.A. so I've still a little time, but what can I do now? You see, I just can't head that delegation to the Minister to try to force my own Head of Department to go back on what he has already decided. I imagine I'm unpopular enough with him as it is without doing that. At the same time, the people really do need a nursery school and they'll want me to head that delegation. After all, I *am* their President. If I refuse, what are they going to think of me?

H

DISCUSSION OF THE CASE

Some members of the group did not want to discuss this case at first as they felt that under no circumstances should a worker accept office in a group to which he or she had responsibilities as a worker. Other members, however, pointed out that the real problem in their opinion was that the people needed a nursery school and that the worker had failed to help them. They would like to study the case in order to reach conclusions about what the worker should have done to help the people with this problem as well as to avoid the personal dilemma that faced her at the end of the case. The group then decided to accept the case for discussion.

Diagnosis

The members of the group thought that the worker was entirely responsible for creating her own dilemma. Her biggest mistake was to allow herself to be elected president of the Association. This, they thought, was bound to put her into an awkward situation whenever, as happened in the case, the members of the Association wanted something done which conflicted with the policy of her Department. Her second mistake was to accept without question the parents' assumption that it was up to the government to provide the nursery school. Her third mistake was to take the lead—through what she said at the School Speech Day—in trying to bring pressure to bear on the Head of her own Department. These three mistakes not only got her into a difficult position with the Head of her Department: they also contributed to her failure to help the parents meet their need for a nursery school.

Implications

All the members of the group agreed that she should not have accepted the presidency of the Association, not only because it was mainly responsible for the dilemma that confronted her at the end of the case, but also because it was inconsistent with her role as community worker. Community workers, members of the group thought, should not accept office in any group with which they worked, partly because they would thereby be depriving some members of the group of a valuable opportunity of acquiring experience in responsible leadership, and partly because it might quite possibly conflict with the worker's real job of encouraging, helping, advising and educating the group's members to develop their own potentialities for thinking and acting for themselves.

Assuming, therefore, that the teacher should not have accepted the presidency, the members of the group went on to consider what she should have done when the members of the Association expressed their need for a nursery school. They thought she could have helped in several ways: e.g. by suggesting:

1. that the members of the Association should make a survey of the need for a nursery school by finding out how many mothers actually went to work; how many of them wanted their children to attend a nursery school; and how many children they had of nursery school age;

2. that there were various ways in which the need revealed by the survey might possibly be met. For example, they might be able to get the government to provide the school; they might as an Association provide the school, either with or without government help; or they might be able to find some qualified person who would be prepared to establish a school on a fee paying basis once the extent of the need for it was known;

3. that although they would obviously prefer the first of these alternatives they should seriously consider the second and third alternatives as well in case the first should prove impracticable.

Had the worker acted in this way, the members of the group felt, she would certainly have avoided getting into difficulties with her Head of Department; and she would also have succeeded in getting the people to think more constructively and realistically about what they could do to help themselves if, as seemed likely, government was unable to help.

CONCLUSIONS

1. *When helping a group to plan a programme or choose a project the worker must try to ensure that every suggestion is adequately considered.*

(One of the conclusions stated at the end of Chapter Three was that the worker must try to ensure that when a project is chosen it will in fact be supported by everyone whose help is needed. The first two cases in this chapter show how sensitive the worker needs to be to the reactions of the group's members if he is to succeed in applying this conclusion to good effect.

Thus it was quite wrong of the worker in Case 20, *The Community Project that Wasn't*, to sit back and watch the schoolmaster take the lead in pushing his piped water scheme through the committee while Mrs. de Souza was quite obviously still unhappy about it; and at the second meeting to do nothing at all to find out whether everyone did in fact agree with the village hall suggestion, and if so whether they were all quite happy about the site. As a result decisions were taken at both meetings with which at least one member did not agree, and it was this that caused the second project to fail. This suggests that when projects are being chosen the worker should be ready to intervene to get any alternative suggestions clearly stated and properly discussed. It is true, of course, that this will tend to slow down the process of decision-making, but this is a small price to pay for increasing the chances that everyone will end by feeling committed to support whatever decision is finally arrived at.)

2. *The worker must at all times try to remain acceptable to all the members.*

(For the worker to be able to intervene successfully in arguments between members he needs considerable skill. In Case 20, *The Community Project that Wasn't*, for instance, he would have needed to intervene in support of Mrs. de Souza's right to have her viewpoint properly discussed without appearing to take her side against the schoolmaster. How a worker can thus intervene without appearing to oppose the viewpoints of other members will be discussed in greater detail in the context of some of the cases included in the next two chapters.)

3. *The worker must avoid appearing to criticize the way the members conduct their meetings.*

(Any attempt on the part of the worker to improve the conduct of meetings may quite easily arouse the resentment of *all* the members against himself. To avoid this risk he needs to remember that he is not a member of the group, but an outsider. If he wishes to be able to continue helping and influencing the group he must above all avoid saying or doing anything that suggests he is critical of the way the members conduct their own affairs: for however much they may disagree among themselves they will be quick to resent such criticism from him. In fact, the greater the inadequacies of the members, the keener their resentment against a critical outsider is likely to be. In trying to help the group, therefore, the worker must always try to relate his suggestions to some good qualities of the group's members, and not to their shortcomings as he did in Case 21, *He Meant Well.*

A worker may sometimes be tempted to try to avoid the disadvantages he suffers as an outsider by participating in the affairs of the group as a member, and preferably as an office-holder. If he does this, however, he tends to get so identified with the purposes of the group that it is difficult for him to provide that kind of detached, *impartial* help that is so often the prime need of the group's members. Moreover, by accepting office he creates expectations on the part of the group's members that are often difficult to reconcile with his duties and responsibilities as a worker. This is well illustrated by Case 22, *The Nursery School,* in which the teacher, by accepting the presidency of a group, identified and involved herself so much in the formulation and execution of its policies that she soon found herself no longer able to reconcile her role as president with that of the job for which she was paid. The worker, it seems, can best serve a group from outside.)

CHAPTER SEVEN

Working with Leaders

In every community and community group there are always some people who by reason of birth, age, education, wealth, occupation, personality and experience, or some other factor, are much more influential than others. It is a recognized principle in community work that the worker should find out who they are, gain their support for his purposes, and as far as possible work with and through them in all he tries to do in their community or group. This principle, however, is more easily stated than applied, and the five cases which follow all illustrate in one way or another the kind of difficulties the worker may have to face when he tries to put this principle into effect.

23. THE SHEIKH AND THE SCHOOLMASTER

The worker fails in his attempts to stimulate a project the younger and more progressive people in a village want.

THE CASE

I was born in a village and have spent all my adult life in villages, first as an assistant teacher in a village school, then as a headmaster, and now for the last few years as a rural community development officer.

The events I am about to relate occurred in a village I had got to know very well. In this village there was a Social Centre which was always well attended by the younger, educated people, and I was in the habit of visiting this centre as often as I could. During these visits I found that many of these people wanted a girls' school established in the village and I was anxious to help them.

I thought the best way to start would be to call a village meeting to consider the matter, so I went along to see the village schoolmaster to get his help in arranging it. While I was talking to him, the village sheikh (religious leader) came in and wanted to know what we were talking about. The schoolmaster seemed reluctant to tell him and immediately turned the conversation to something else.

When the sheikh had gone, we continued our discussion and in the end decided that it would be better to start by putting our idea to the village development committee. I therefore invited the members of this committee to meet me at the school to discuss the idea, and to this meeting I also invited the sheikh. The sheikh, however, sent a messenger to say he was not well.

However, although the sheikh did not come to the meeting, the others came and agreed to support the idea. The next step, they thought, should be to hold a full village meeting at which I could talk about the new project and show a film to help the people to understand how useful a girls' school would be. They decided to hold this meeting also at the school.

I arrived at the school in good time. The schoolmaster and his pupils were there, but none of the village people. However, the schoolmaster assured me that the people would come as soon as they heard the commentary to the film start up, so I started showing the film but still no one came. In fact, the meeting never took place at all. I found out afterwards that the sheikh had told all the people not to go to the meeting as the cinema was a bad thing and the work of the devil. After that I could not do anything more in that village and the project therefore failed.

DISCUSSION OF THE CASE

The members of the group which discussed this case thought that the situation in this village was typical of that in very many other villages, in that the effect of the school had been to create a rift between the younger and more progressive people who had been to school and the older and more traditionally-minded people who felt like the sheikh. These older people, they thought, and more particularly the sheikh, were feeling threatened by the changes that were taking place around them, and very suspicious of the motives of the people, such as the schoolmaster and the community development officer, who had been mainly responsible for introducing them.

The members of the group thought that if the community development officer had been as interested in meeting the older people in the community as he was in the younger people who attended the Social Centre, he would have been aware of the strength of these feelings, and also of the extent of the influence of the sheikh.

He might then have acted very differently. As it was, however, he greatly underestimated the sheikh's influence, if
indeed he was aware of it at all, with the result that almost
everything he did or did not do had the effect of further
antagonizing him: his choice of project (he chose the one least
likely to find favour with the sheikh); his initial approach
to the schoolmaster to the neglect of the sheikh; his acquiescence
in the schoolmaster's rudeness to the sheikh when the sheikh
called at his house; his subsequent neglect to recognize the
sheikh's status as a village leader by calling on him to explain
the project and seek his support *before* the meeting of the village
development committee; and even the decision to hold this
meeting at the school. The cumulative effect of all these real or
imagined slights, members of the group felt, must have been to
make the sheikh determined to do his best to make the project fail.

The sheikh, they thought, behaved very intelligently. He
avoided the community development officer's meeting with
the village development committee, they suggested, not
because he was ill, but because if he had attended it he would
either have had to oppose the project openly—which he may
not have wished to do with the community development officer
present: or remain silent—in which case he might appear, like
Mrs. de Souza in Case 20, to have agreed with the decisions
taken. By staying away from the meeting he left himself
free to disassociate himself from any or all of the decisions
the committee had taken, and by choosing to attack the
committee's decision to show a film at the village meeting, he
attacked at the point where his influence was strongest, and
without directly attacking the project itself. Such an attack
might have been harder to justify.

Implications

The members of the group felt that the worker in this case
had a very limited idea of what his role in the community
should be. They agreed that it was his job to introduce change,
but felt that he should always try hard to ensure that the change
would be acceptable to everyone. This the worker had not done.

By associating mainly with the younger people who already wanted change, and by neglecting the older, traditionally-minded people who did not see the need for it, not only was he increasing the risk of the kind of failure which happened in this case, he was also helping to disrupt the community by widening the gap between young and old within it. What he had most needed to do, but had not done, was to establish friendly relationships with the older people in the hope of educating them to understand the need for some development: and, since the sheikh was likely to be the most influential of their leaders, he should have done all he could to become friendly with him and win his support.

The members of the group recognized that this would have involved the community development officer in much slow and difficult work, but felt that this above all was the work that most needed to be done. Had the worker realized this, they thought he would have behaved very differently. He would have spent rather less time at the Social Centre, and more in making friendly visits to the sheikh. Then, when he wanted to broach the subject of the girls' school, he should have made a point of recognizing the sheikh's superior community status by seeking his support before he went to see the schoolmaster. If he had done this he would have had a much better chance of getting the sheikh to consider the idea on its merits: and, if the sheikh had genuine doubts about the desirability of the scheme, he would have had a chance of seeing how, if at all, they could be overcome. He would then be in a much better position to decide whether to go ahead with the scheme or not.

24. THE CHIEF OF IKAM

A chief who feels he has been slighted withdraws his promise to allocate land for a farm settlement scheme.

THE CASE

In my country many of the youths who have been to school have learnt to despise tilling the soil as their fathers do, but yet cannot

get any other kind of work. Therefore most of them do nothing but
laze their time away.

My government wanted to deal with this problem and had the
idea of establishing farm settlements where young men of this kind
would be taught up-to-date farming methods in the hope that they
would then work on the land. One of these settlements was to be
established for the youths of Ikam, a town in my area.

The town of Ikam is in the middle of a tribal area of the same
name, and the chief of the tribe lives there. Nowadays he has much
less authority in the town than he had even a few years ago, because
some of his powers have been handed over to a council elected by the
people living in the town: but he is still greatly respected by the
people and still retains his traditional rights over unallocated tribal
land. I was therefore instructed to ask the chief to allocate 800 acres
of unused tribal land for this purpose.

I arranged to see him and took with me to the meeting the
people's chosen councillors from the town. I explained the project
very carefully and everyone at the meeting was all in favour of it.
The chief promised to provide 800 acres on a good site near the
town, and the town's councillors promised to get it cleared by the
communal labour of the people.

I came away from that meeting feeling very happy. I met the
town's councillors the next day and they formed a sub-committee to
mark out the land and make arrangements to have it cleared. All
of us went into the bush, saw the land, and marked it out. The
councillors said that the townspeople would be ready to start clearing the land in four days' time.

On the appointed day I went along to see the work begin, but to
my great surprise I found that no one was willing to work. The
reason was that the chief had sent word to the people that they were
not to clear the land as his consent had not been obtained. This, of
course, was simply not true. What had really happened was that he
had quarrelled with the members of the town council because they
had not sent him the customary token present in recognition of his
gift of tribal land. But then why should they? The chief was not
giving it to them. He was merely allocating it in the general interest
of the members of the tribe.

DISCUSSION OF THE CASE
Diagnosis

Some of the members of the group which discussed this case
started by feeling that the community development officer
was in no way responsible for the trouble that arose. They

thought it unlikely that he was himself a member of the Ikam tribe, and it was therefore unreasonable to expect him to know all the details of Ikam tribal custom. Most or all of the members of the Ikam town council, however, must have been members of the tribe. They would know their local tribal custom and they, if anyone, were to blame for ignoring it.

Most members of the group, on the other hand, felt that the community development officer was at least partly responsible. He must have known that the chief had recently lost a good deal of his former authority over the people in the town, and he could therefore have foreseen that he would naturally be anxious to safeguard the powers he still had. He might also have suspected that the councillors, or at any rate some of the more 'progressive' ones, would be quite eager to increase their status at the expense of the chief. He should therefore have been on his guard against the kind of trouble that actually arose. In the view of these members of the group this was part of the job he was paid to do. After some further discussion this was agreed by all members of the group.

Implications

The members of the group then discussed what they thought the community development officer should have done, but found it very difficult to agree. Two members had very little sympathy with the chief. They felt he was a useless relic of the past who was using his remaining influence in order to prevent much needed progress. In their view, the community development officer should have exerted all possible pressure on the chief to make him keep his promise to give the land. He could have done this, they thought, by threatening to report adversely on him to the central government. They also thought that the community development officer should have urged the members of the town council to try to persuade the people that the chief was in the wrong; that the central government was on their side; and that they could safely support their own elected members by going ahead with the clearing of the land.

The rest of the group strongly disagreed. The fact that the

people had not turned out to work, they said, showed that the influence of the chief was still much stronger than that of the councillors in the town, and that any further attack on the status of the chief was likely to make things worse. Moreover, they thought that the chief had right on his side.

This led to a long discussion about what the community development officer should alternatively have done. It was generally agreed that he needed to make the chief feel that both he and the councillors fully recognized his status, and that to do this he needed to ensure that the customary present was duly given. If he had first briefed himself in local tribal custom concerning the allocation of land (which he should have done since he was taking the initiative in asking for it) he would have known that it should be given, and it was then up to him to make sure that it *was* given. At this point there was some discussion about how he could do this if the town councillors did not see the need for it. Everyone recognized that he could not make them, but thought that the councillors would, in fact, have agreed once the likely consequences of not doing so had been pointed out to them.

This was the main point, but some other suggestions were also made which some members thought would have helped to ensure the goodwill of the chief. Thus one suggestion was that the community development officer should have seen the chief to ask for his support before contacting the councillors; and another that he should have kept the chief informed, or got the councillors to keep him informed, about the decisions they subsequently made. The group, however, did not attempt to decide whether these ideas were good or not. So much, they thought, would depend on what was customary behaviour. What they did agree on, however, was that the community development officer should have himself behaved, and tried to get the council members to behave, acceptably in accordance with tribal custom in all their dealings with the chief.

25. THE NEW VILLAGE HALL

The members of a once flourishing community association begin to quarrel when they start using their new village hall.

THE CASE

A village Community Association in my district had been in the habit of holding its meetings in a shed which belonged to its Chairman, but as its membership increased and its activities grew it decided to build a real village hall.

The secretary of the Association's executive committee invited me to a meeting to help them decide what to do. They said they had been thinking of knocking down the existing shed in order to put up a bigger and better building on the same site: and they asked me to support their application for a grant.

I told them I would do my best to get them a grant, and was sure they could get one if their Chairman would agree to sell or lease them the site. This was necessary as no grant could be made for a building on privately owned land. The Chairman then said he was quite willing to sell the land. In due course the ownership of the site was transferred, the grant was made, and I was able to help the committee with the plans. Everyone worked with a will and the building was soon finished. It was a proud day for the community, and for me, when they opened their fine new hall.

Trouble, however, was not long in coming, and I was there when it came. A Mr. Harris started it just as the Chairman was on the point of ending a Council meeting. 'I've got a point I want to make, Mr. Chairman,' he said, 'and it concerns the use of this hall. I'm supposed to have it on Tuesdays for my Youth Club, but you told me, Sir, that I couldn't have it last week because you had reserved it for your Church Council meeting. It has happened to others too, and I want something done about it.' Then another member, a Mr. Martin, backed him up by saying that although the hall was now the community's hall, the Chairman still seemed to think it belonged to him!

The Chairman looked very upset and tried to justify what he had done. 'To take Mr. Harris's point first', he said, 'I would have thought that even he would agree that the Church Council is more important than the youth club; and as for Mr. Martin what he says is just another proof that one can't please everyone. I can only say that I've always done my best.'

This satisfied neither Mr. Harris nor Mr. Martin. They were sure that people in other villages managed this kind of thing much better, and appealed to me for support. I had to say, of course, that most village community halls were run by a management committee. Most of the Council's members thought this a good idea and voted in favour of it.

You might have thought that this would have ended the matter, but unfortunately it did not, for the Chairman took the vote as a personal slight, resigned from the Council, and took no further interest in it. This split the community, for many people felt that the Council had treated the Chairman very badly in view of all he had done to help the Association in the past. Thus the Association lost many of its members. Eventually, there were scarcely any activities still taking place in the hall, and even those that were left were poorly supported. I had expected that hall to be a real blessing, but it has caused nothing but trouble.

DISCUSSION OF THE CASE

Diagnosis

The members of the group which discussed this case felt sorry for the worker, who, they agreed, had done nothing very obviously wrong. Nevertheless, the case began with a flourishing community association and ended with it nearly dead. In one way or another, therefore, the worker had failed.

The cause of the trouble seemed clear enough. The Chairman was probably quite the most influential man in the community —kind, generous, public-spirited, and well liked by nearly everyone; but also paternalistic in his attitude to the community, used to having his own way, and quite unused to having his actions and decisions questioned. No one in the community association objected to this attitude while they depended on him for somewhere to meet, but some members did object to it once the association had succeeded in getting a hall of its own. The cause of the trouble, therefore, was that the Chairman did not change his attitude when the situation changed. He still continued to act as when he owned the shed.

If the worker had foreseen this problem before the new hall was built, he might have been able to deal with it, but he did not foresee it. This was because he was so preoccupied with helping the people with their project that he never even

onsidered what effect it might eventually have on the attitudes
nd relationships of the association's members. Had he done
o, he would have realized the need to try to do something.

mplications

What he needed to have done, the members of the group
hought, was to change the Chairman's attitude, which was
ut-of-date, and to change it before the new hall was built.
ut they found it hard to agree on *how* he could have done it.
hey discussed this for a long time, some members suggesting
hat he should have seen the Chairman on his own, and others
eling that he should have tackled the problem at a meeting
f the Council. In the end the latter view prevailed. His best
hance, they thought, was when he told the Council that in
rder to get a grant for their building they would have to own
he site. He could then have pointed out that the new building
ould also be the property of the Council and not, as heretofore,
he personal property of the Chairman; that this would involve
ertain changes; and, in particular, that the Council would
o longer be able to leave the Chairman to bear the whole
urden of managing the hall. He could then have suggested
hat they might agree to do what other villages already did,
hich was to appoint a management committee to run the hall.

If he had done this, the members of the group thought, there
ould have been a good chance that the Chairman would
ave been willing to accept it, since he would not have felt, as
e did later on, that he was being personally attacked. If on
he other hand he had opposed this suggestion, and even
efused to lease or sell the site unless he retained full control—
nd members of the group thought this very unlikely—he
ould have lost the sympathy of nearly everyone in the com-
unity, and the Council would probably have been able to go
head with the new building on some other site.

While every member basically agreed with this approach,
me felt that the worker should have done even more to safe-
uard and enhance the Chairman's status, for this they thought
as the key to the solution of the problem. They suggested,

for instance, that the worker should have encouraged the Council members to recognize the help their Chairman had given them in every way they could: by arranging, for example a public ceremony at which he could hand over the title to the site; by referring to his generosity in speeches at the opening of the hall; and even, as one member suggested, by naming the new hall after him. Other members, however, thought that this would be going too far and felt that the worker might quite easily cause trouble if he allowed himself to make suggestions of this kind.

26. THE WOULD-BE BENEFACTORS

An agricultural extension officer meets unexpected trouble after helping a village council choose a nursery site for a seedling nursery of its own.

THE CASE

Last year I was trying to get the farmers in my district to plant more fruit trees. I was quite successful in most villages, but made little progress in the village of San Pedro because it was so far away from the provincial nursery that it was hard for the people to get supplies of good fruiting stock. I therefore suggested to their village council that they might like to establish a small nursery of their own. They thought this a very good idea if only they could find a suitable site.

A couple of weeks later their chairman wrote in to say that two members of the Council, a Mr. Degas and a Mr. Bart, had both generously offered to give a site and that the Council would like my advice about which one to choose. The Council was meeting again in three days' time and he suggested that I might go out early to inspect the sites before the meeting began.

Well, I went out, inspected the sites, and decided on the one preferred. At the meeting I congratulated the members of the Council on their decision to establish a nursery of their own, and on having on their Council two such public-spirited gentlemen as Mr. Degas and Mr. Bart. I then said that I had carefully inspected the two sites and had decided in favour of that offered by Mr. Bart. 'It has just the kind of well-drained sandy loam that young seedlings like,' I said, 'and it has a well that can supply water during the dry season. Mr. Degas's site has a good soil too, but it's a bit heavier and down there by the stream there's always a danger of flooding.'

Then the trouble started, for Mr. Degas at once began arguing against my choice. 'It's all very well,' he said, 'for this officer to look around today and say that this site is better than that, but we've lived here all our lives and I, for one, don't agree with him. I doubt very much whether that well of Mr. Bart's will be able to supply all the water the nursery will need in the hot weather: and as for his talk about the danger of my site being flooded, I've never had any flood water there since the channel was cleared.'

This started a heated argument between the two men. I did what I could to smooth things over and in the end most of the council members came round to my way of thinking and voted in favour of Bart's site. Then we got down to making arrangements for work to start and this went through smoothly enough. In fact, Mr. Degas never said another word. But although I've put a lot of work into this project since, it has never really got going. To be quite honest, it's a complete flop and I wish I'd never started it. I can't prove it, of course, but I'm sure that Degas has been stirring up trouble. He's got a lot of friends in that village and I don't think he's ever forgiven me for choosing Bart's site rather than his. Yet after all I only gave my honest opinion, and if I'd said that Degas's site was better then Bart would have made trouble. So what else could I have done?

DISCUSSION OF THE CASE
Diagnosis

The members of the group which discussed this case found it easy to diagnose the cause of the trouble. Degas and Bart, they thought, were rivals for community status. This was at least partly the reason why each had offered a site and was anxious to have his offer accepted. They also thought that the chairman and other members of the Council were aware of this and did not want to have to choose between them for fear of causing trouble. This was a strong additional reason for them wanting the worker to give his expert opinon, but all the worker succeeded in doing by giving it was to cause the trouble and get involved in it himself.

Implications

The implications of this diagnosis, however, were much harder to work out, for whichever site was chosen, and whoever chose it, it seemed that there was bound to be trouble.

Some members of the group almost gave up at this point.

I

The best the worker could hope for, they said, was to keep out
of trouble himself, and this he could do by refusing to choose
between the sites. But, in the view of other members, this would
also have caused trouble. After all, as they pointed out, he had
been responsible for suggesting the nursery project in the first
place; he was an expert; and the Council had asked for his
help. Therefore he simply *had* to do something.

At this point one member suggested that the worker could
have given advice without going so far as to choose the site,
and that this was in fact was what he ought to have done. It was
true that the worker was an expert, but this did not mean that
he was an expert in everything. What he did know better than
the Council members were the conditions of soil, sunlight or
shade, drainage, and freedom from flooding that the young
seedlings would need. What he could not know nearly so well
was which of the two sites was actually better, as this would
partly depend on knowledge of local conditions. The members
of the Council were likely to be better judges of this than he was
because they were local men. Only they, for instance, were
likely to know whether the well on Bart's site really did run
dry in the hot season, and whether Degas's site was ever in
any real danger of flooding.

Another member suggested that apart from these purely
technical factors the choice of site might be influenced by other
factors too. Distance from the village might be one such factor,
for instance, and easy access from a motor road might be
another.

Following up this idea, the members of the group agreed
that the worker should not have committed himself to choosing
one of the sites, nor even to inspect the sites before the meeting.
His best hope, they thought, would have been to list and explain
each of the characteristics a good nursery should have; stress
to the Council members that the success of the project would
largely depend on their making a good choice; and suggest
that they inspect the two sites in order to assess the advantages
or disadvantages of each site against each point on the list.
Involving the whole group in making a thorough and objective

assessment of this kind, the members of the group thought, would have many advantages. No choice would have been made until all the Council members, including Degas and Bart, had made a thorough study of all the pros and cons of each site for themselves, and whatever decision they finally arrived at, they would all feel more committed to it because they had assessed the facts for themselves. Of course, the owner of the site which was not chosen would still be unhappy, but the members of the group thought that he would certainly have had less cause for resentment against the worker, and less scope for causing trouble in the community afterwards than he had in the case.

Some members also suggested that any resentment he felt might still have been overcome had the worker been able to suggest some good alternative community use for his site.

CONCLUSIONS

1. *The worker needs to give as much or more attention to leaders who do not sympathize with his aims as to those who do.*

(From the worker's standpoint, a community's leaders are the people who have, or can exert, a significant influence on the opinions and behaviour of others. It is because they have this influence that the worker needs so much to get their support. Even if only one of several leaders is against a project he may cause it to fail, and the greater his influence is, the more likely this failure will be.

This suggests that the worker should give as much or more attention to leaders who do not sympathize with his aims as to those who do, but he does not always see his problem in this light. He may in fact be tempted to work mainly, if not exclusively, with those who sympathize with his aims, and to neglect unduly those who do not. Most community leaders, however, are very sensitive about their status, and by working with one leader and not with another the worker is in effect recognizing the status of the one and not of the other. This is nearly always a mistake. By avoiding the less co-operative leader, the worker suffers in two ways: on the one hand, he is likely to arouse such a leader's resentment against himself; and on the other, he loses many much-needed opportunities of educating him and gaining his support. This is well illustrated by what happened in Case 23, *The Sheikh and the Schoolmaster*, when the worker underestimated the power of the sheikh and antagonized him by working through the schoolmaster. Much the same happened in Case 24, *The Chief of Ikam*, as a result of the worker underestimating the influence of the traditional chief and failing to ensure appropriate recognition of his status. This suggests that the worker should aim to work with, and award appropriate status to, *every* community leader, however uncooperative he may initially be, and however troublesome it may be to work with him.

The worker needs to be specially careful in this respect because his task is often complicated by one leader trying to enhance his own community status by 'capturing' the worker for himself. This, for example, might go far to explain why the schoolmaster was so reluctant to tell the sheikh what he and the worker were talking about in Case 23.)

2. *The worker must ensure that in promoting change he adequately safeguards the status of the community's traditional leaders.*

(Development, i.e. the changes that the community worker tries to stimulate and encourage, will often face the traditional and paternalistic type of leader with the need to adapt himself not only to such new ideas as education for girls (as in Case 23, *The Sheikh and the Schoolmaster*), but also to a different concept of himself as leader (as in Case 25, *The New Village Hall*). It is one of the jobs of the worker to try to foresee the need for changes of this kind and then to help the leader himself to recognize the need for change, in the hope that he may change his attitude as the new situation requires. And the key to success in this, as in all other work with leaders, is to do everything possible to ensure that the change does not adversely affect the leader's status.)

3. *The worker must avoid appearing to favour any one leader at the expense of any rival leaders.*

(In Case 26, *The Would-be Benefactors*, the worker has to deal with two competing leaders. Since the status of both leaders is involved, whatever he decides will please the one but is bound to antagonize the other. This is the commonest, and most difficult, of all the problems the worker has to meet, but the conclusion is clear. If he wishes to work with the *whole* community, and therefore in harmony with *all* its leaders, he must somehow avoid favouring one at the expense of the other. He must therefore behave as a neutral, but this does not mean that he will do nothing. It is still his job to help the community to decide, but he must do this, not by deciding in favour of one against the other, but by helping everyone concerned systematically and objectively to consider the pros and cons of the different viewpoints in order to assess how the interest of the *whole* community can best be served. This function of the worker will be studied in greater detail in the next chapter.)

CHAPTER EIGHT

Dealing with Faction

THE cases in this chapter, like those in the previous chapter, present problems of working with leaders, but are of a different and more difficult kind. This is because the leaders in the cases which follow are not so much community leaders as leaders of *factions* within the community. As such they are less concerned with promoting the good of the whole community than with advancing the particular sectional interests of their own faction against those of other factions. It is this which makes the worker's task of trying to get them to work together for the good of the community so difficult.

27. THE RIVAL LEADERS

A trainee-worker is sent to a village to get practical experience during training. He succeeds in starting a project but fails to get it completed.

THE CASE

During my training at a community development training centre, I was sent to a small village of about two hundred and fifty people with instructions to live there for three months. During that time I was to try to organize a youth club and some evening classes for adults. I was also told to try to stimulate the villagers to undertake some kind of community project.

This village had no village council, but only a headman elected by the people to be their representative in dealing with the government authorities. This headman had been elected not long before I went there. He had been told that I would be coming and had promised the Principal of my Centre to give me all the help he could. So when I arrived, the first thing I did was to go to see him and explain what I had been told to do. He welcomed me very kindly, provided me with a room in which to sleep, and called a village meeting so that everyone could hear what I had to say.

The people seemed very pleased when they heard why I had come, and they were particularly pleased with the idea of attending some evening classes. They said, however, that they had no room in the village big enough for this purpose, and offered to build a community hall in which the classes could meet if the Principal of my training centre would help by providing some of the materials they would need.

When I told them a few days later that my Principal had agreed to do this on condition that they would provide the site and do all the work, they were very happy and work started almost at once: but after only a few days no one would work any more. I then discovered that there were two leaders in that village, both of whom had stood for election as headman, and that the defeated leader now hated the leader who had defeated him. I also learnt that neither he nor his followers had attended the meeting at which the building of the hall had been agreed, and that they were now threatening harm to anyone who helped to build it. This was why all work on the building had so quickly stopped.

I tried very hard to get work started on the building again, and the headman tried hard too, but the people were too afraid to do anything and the building was never finished. Was I bound to fail or might I have succeeded if I had acted differently?

Diagnosis   DISCUSSION OF THE CASE

The group which studied this case first discussed why the defeated leader and his followers acted as they did. Two suggestions were put forward: the one, that unlike the headman and his followers they did not want a community hall; and the other, that they opposed this project, as they would have opposed any other project decided on by the headman and his followers, simply and solely to revenge themselves for their leader's defeat at the recent election. The group quickly rejected the first of these suggestions. Only the second, members of the group felt, could satisfactorily explain the absence of the rival faction from the village meeting and the action it subsequently took to frighten people into abandoning work on the building.

Although the situation was a very difficult one, the members of the group thought that the trainee-worker contributed significantly to his own failure. They noted, for instance, that he seemed to have started work without first having made a preliminary survey or study of any kind, and that he therefore remained in complete ignorance of the existence of faction in that community until he inquired why work on the building had stopped. Had he tried much harder to get to know the community better from the start, he would have become aware of the existence of faction much earlier. He would then have avoided the mistake of assuming that the village meeting was fully representative, and he would presumably have done something to try to get the rival faction to co-operate.

Implications

Having agreed on this diagnosis, the members of the group went on to discuss what the worker should have done. They all agreed that since faction occurs in so many villages and so often causes projects to fail, the worker should have been on the look-out for it. They felt that he should already have got a sufficient general knowledge of the village before he went into it to know that a new headman had recently been elected; and that if he had inquired further he could easily have found out that there was a defeated candidate who might or might not be resentful, but who anyway was likely to be an influential local leader who would need to be contacted as well as the headman. They thought that he could have got this information, and other useful information besides, if he had first visited the headquarters of the district in which the village was situated and called on some of the departmental field officers of, for example, the agricultural, health, co-operative, or local government departments likely to be stationed there. Some of these officers could almost certainly have briefed him about the situation in the village before he ever went to it.

But if he had thus become aware of the existence of faction, or even merely felt that he had good reason for suspecting it before he arrived at the village, what then could he have done? The members of the group discussed this at length before agreeing:

1. that he should have tried to get the village headman to agree to postpone, for a few days at least, the village meeting he proposed to call; and

2. that he should have used this time

    (*a*) to get on friendly terms with some of the village people, and more especially with their leaders;

    (*b*) to find out what needs they had as a community and what he could do to help them meet them; and

    (*c*) to try to get the various leaders to sink their factional differences in order to co-operate with him and with each other for the common good.

The members of the group then spent some time discussing how he could best do this: by seeing each faction leader separately? by seeing them together? or by seeing them together with other influential people who were not strongly attached to either faction? In the end, most members felt that if they had had to tackle this problem they would have preferred to talk in the first place to each of the faction leaders separately, either alone or together with a few of his followers. This, they thought, would have made it easier for them to create an informal friendly atmosphere in which it would have been easier for each leader to talk frankly without initially publicly committing himself for or against any particular viewpoint. The worker's job would be to try to find some basis acceptable to both leaders on which they could agree to support some *one* project which would demonstrably benefit everyone. Only when the worker felt that he had really found such a basis, members of the group felt, should he risk bringing the leaders together at a full village meeting for public discussion of such a project: for if they quarrelled publicly at such a meeting the worker would have destroyed whatever chance he may once have had of getting them to agree to work together.

The members of the group did not feel very hopeful about the worker's chance of success even if he had tried to work in the way they had suggested, although they thought he would at any rate have done less harm. Even an experienced worker, they thought, would have found this a very difficult situation to tackle, and one which would have needed plenty of time: whereas the worker in the case was a trainee, young and inexperienced, and posted to work in the community for only three months.

This made the group very critical of the training centre which had sent him to get his first practical experience of community development work in such a difficult community situation. They thought that no trainee should be posted to start up new work in a community which he would have to leave after only three months, and certainly not in a community which was already divided by faction. They also thought that every trainee should be briefed, or at any rate trained to brief himself, about the community to which he is to be posted *before* he actually starts work in it; that he should be sent to a community in which some work has already been done; and that he should he helped and supervised in his work by the local field worker to whose area he has been posted as well as by visits made by the training staff. Neglect of all these points in this case, the group felt, had not only resulted in a most unhappy and probably harmful experience for the trainee worker, but had probably also worsened the conflict situation within the community by intensifying the rift between the two factions.

28. THE MAJORITY VOTE

A village council consists of representatives of two opposing factions. One faction succeeds in narrowly outvoting the other in favour of its own project. The defeated faction retaliates by refusing to help and the project fails.

THE CASE

The events I shall describe took place in a community divided by a river which also separated the adherents of two different religions. The river, however, was crossed by a bridge. All the people had the same government-appointed headman; and all their children attended the same school. The young boys from both sides played games in friendly competition. The boys from the north side would serenade the girls on the south side and *vice versa*. But each religious group had its own church and celebrated its feast days independently, and on these occasions each attempted to outdo the other by trying to attract the greater number of distinguished visitors.

I was appointed to work in the district which included this village, and one of my jobs was to get the people in as many villages as possible to agree to elect village councils or project committees. I therefore called the people of this particular village to a meeting and persuaded them to elect a council. To this council they elected an equal number of members from each religious group. However, the council members could never agree on a single project. Whatever one group suggested was opposed by the other, which had an equal number of votes.

One day one member of one group was absent, and the opposing group took advantage of this to pass (by a majority of one!) a resolution in favour of building a community centre on their side of the river. I endorsed this majority decision and forwarded to my head office an application for a government grant. This was approved, but when the time came for the people to start work, the group which had been outvoted refused to co-operate, while the members of the group which had passed the resolution were unable to provide enough labour and materials by themselves. I tried hard to reconcile the two groups but without success. In the end I had to write in to headquarters cancelling the application for a grant.

DISCUSSION OF THE CASE

The problem was first very briefly discussed to ensure that everyone had got it clear. It was agreed that although the worker had succeeded in his immediate purpose which, as stated in the case, was to establish a representative village council or project committee, he had failed in his real purpose which was to get the people working together on self-help projects for the good of their community. Indeed, the members of the group felt that he had done actual harm. They noted that whereas at the beginning of the case the people, though divided, had been getting on quite well together, at the end of it they were much more seriously divided. Thus all the worker had actually achieved was to worsen relationships between the two groups.

The members then had discussions in small groups to diagnose just why the worker failed and to suggest how he could have tackled his job better. When the main group reformed, the reports of the sub-groups were considered and certain points were agreed.

Diagnosis

The group agreed on three main points as follows:

(*a*) that the worker had completely failed to appreciate the significance in relation to his purpose of the people's existing religious divisions;

(*b*) that he had persuaded the people to elect a village council (which was easy), without making any serious attempts to help either the people or the council members to agree on common aims (which was more difficult); and

(*c*) that he had acted on a majority decision of the council although he knew that half of the people in the village strongly disagreed with it; and that he did this because he was more interested in material results than in the feelings, attitudes, and relationships among the people.

Implications

The members of the group felt that the worker should have assessed the situation much more carefully before doing anything. They thought that he should have consulted other government officers in the district who had worked in this community before: and that he could have found out a good deal more from the local political and religious leaders, the chairman and officers of local groups, and the schoolteachers. Some members also thought that he should have sounded the opinions of people in neighbouring communities. They thought that the worker might get a truer and less biased picture from people who knew the community but were not members of it.

Had he made any real attempt to assess local relationships, the group felt, he could hardly have failed to realize that his first task must be to help the two groups to find purposes they could both share. Until he succeeded in this, no project committee or council was likely to be effective.

The group felt that he could have tackled this task in several ways, each of which was then discussed.

(*a*) *He could have attempted it at a village meeting.* After some discussion most of the group's members became increasingly uneasy about attempting to deal with the problem in this way. They considered whether he should take responsibility for organizing the meeting himself, and if so how he should decide on the time, place, and other arrangements for the meeting; or whether he should leave it to some local people to organize. If so, which local people should he approach, and how could he be sure that they would make arrangements acceptable to everyone so that all the leaders of both groups would attend? Also, who should chair the meeting? A local leader? But every leader belonged to one or other of the two religious groups. The Government headman? But was he liked and trusted by the people? An outside dignitary? But was one available who knew the community well and was equally liked and trusted by both groups? Until the worker was able to find the right answer to all these questions, the group thought, holding a meeting might easily do more harm than good.

(b) *He could have attempted it on a training course for village leaders.* The member who had introduced the problem had told the group that the community development workers in his organization could call in a specialist training officer to conduct courses of village leader training. Such courses brought together leaders from several villages to think about what was needed in their villages and how these various needs could best be met, as well as teaching them how to conduct their village council meetings more efficiently. Such courses usually lasted for two whole days or four half-days. The group then considered whether a course of this kind would have helped the worker to solve his problem.

Most members of the group felt that this was a much more hopeful line of approach. In particular, they felt that the presence on the course of leaders from other (less divided?) communities would be a helpful factor, but they also felt that two days was too short a time in which to produce a lasting change in the attitudes to each other of the leaders of the two religious groups. The best that could be hoped for, they thought, was that it might start a process which the worker could afterwards complete. They were interested, too, in the respective

functions of the training officer and the community development worker. Although the training officer was a specialist
and senior in status, they felt that *on the course* he should function
as helper and adviser to the worker. They felt that this was
important on several counts. The training officer was an
expert only in training techniques. He did not know the local
leaders and knew nothing about their purely local problems.
In this field the local worker was, or should have been, the
expert, and for this reason he should have major responsibility
for decisions affecting the content and conduct of the course.
They also though that this would enhance his prestige with the
village leaders, and this, they felt, was very desirable.

(*c*) *He could have attempted it at the village council meetings.*
Most members thought that a training course would not solve
the worker's problem for him completely. They felt that the
final solution had to be reached in the village council meetings,
and that the worker should therefore have attended them
regularly. At such meetings he should have set himself the task
of helping and encouraging the leaders of the two groups to
reach specific agreements—however limited in scope—on what
they might do *together or separately* to improve local amenities
and local community life.

29. THE DISTRICT COUNCILLOR

The worker wants a representative committee set up to
manage a village literacy class. He fails because the leader of a
village faction insists that if the class is started he will manage
it himself.

THE CASE

As a community development officer it is one of my jobs to get adult
literacy classes started in the villages. There is no real difficulty about
this in the ordinary way for most of the people are very keen on
learning to read and write. Indeed, in many villages the people
themselves send in to ask for help. All I have to do is to visit the
village as soon as I can to find out how many people want to learn
and whether there is anyone willing to teach; arrange to supply the
necessary primers and show the teacher how to use them; and get

he people to agree to set up a small representative committee to nrol the learners, fix the time and place for the class to meet, and nake any other purely local arrangements, such as lighting if the lass is to meet after dark.

One day one of the elected members of our local government ouncil called at my office to invite me to visit his village where, he aid, there was a young man willing to teach and plenty of people ager to learn. Of course, I agreed to go and a few days later we vent out together to meet the elders of the village.

I was warmly greeted when I arrived. It was obvious that the eople were keen enough and all went well at the meeting until I aid that they would need to appoint a small committee to manage he class and that this committee should be as representative as ossible of the various village groups.

Immediately there was trouble. There were two party political rganizations in the village and the district councillor was the ocally elected representative of one of them. He now strongly bjected to the other party political group having anything to do vith the running of the literacy class. It had been his idea to have a lass, he said, and he and his friends were perfectly well able to nanage it. This started an argument with the supporters of the ther party which I tried to stop by pointing out that managing a iteracy class had nothing whatever to do with politics, but that if ne party was to be represented on the management committee hen the other must be represented also.

Then one of the elders said that there were two churches in the illage, each of which had its own school. He agreed that the com- nittee should be representative and thought, therefore, that both f these churches should be represented on the committee as well as oth political parties. But, he said, even if they were there would till be trouble. The class would have to meet somewhere, and prob- bly at one of the schools, but whichever school was chosen he was ertain that the people belonging to the other church would not ome. He therefore suggested that there should be two classes, one t each school.

At this point I remarked that I had no objection to there being a lass at each school if there were enough learners to be divided into wo classes and if a second teacher could be found. This would be omething for the committee to decide.

I stayed on for a long time while the elders argued and quarrelled vith one another, but whatever I did I could not get them to agree. That district councillor and his supporters belonged to the same church as well as to the same party and were determined not to have representatives of the other party and the other church on the management committee. As for me, I told them that I was anxious to help but that there was nothing I could do until they could first agree among themselves. This they would not or could not do and there is still no literacy class in that village. Now that district councillor has blamed me. They could have had a literacy class, he said, but for the fact that I came out in support of the other side!

DISCUSSION OF THE CASE

Diagnosis

From what was stated in the case, it appeared to the group that the worker had a fixed idea of what he had to do to establish literacy classes in the villages and always followed the same pattern. This was

(a) to find out how many people wanted to learn to read and write;

(b) to inquire about teachers;

(c) to arrange to supply primers and train the teachers; and

(d) to get a representative management committee established and instructed in its duties.

The group noted that this approach had apparently worked very successfully on previous occasions but noted, too, that its success depended on the willingness of the people to appoint such a committee. It had failed in the present case because, although the people undoubtedly wanted a literacy class, they were so divided by party political and religious faction that one of the faction leaders, the district councillor, was determined not to allow the leaders of the other faction any share in managing it. This, the group thought, was because he wanted to get all the credit for getting the class started for himself and his party.

The members of the group agreed that the district councillor's attitude made things very difficult for the worker, but they also thought that faction was such a common source of difficulty in community work that the worker should always have been on the look-out for it and ready to deal with it whenever it might occur. In this case, however, the worker was not on the

ook-out for it. Thus he went to the village quite unaware of
the existence of faction and expecting to get the people to
appoint a representative committee in that village as easily
as in other villages. Therefore he was quite unprepared for
the trouble when it came, and completely failed to deal with
it when it did come. In fact, it was he who sparked off the
trouble by saying that a representative committee must be
appointed to manage the class, and he then made matters worse
by insisting that nothing could be done until this committee
was set up. The result of all this was that

(*a*) no literacy class was started;
(*b*) the two factions quarrelled with each other so openly that
there was now very little chance of getting a literacy class
or any other project started for a long time to come; and
(*c*) the worker had made himself disliked by the district
councillor's faction. This, the group felt, was bound to
affect adversely any future attempt he might make to
work in that community.

The group thought that he could probably have done much
better than he did if he had made himself aware of the true
state of affairs in the village before he went to the meeting or,
if that were not possible, had thought out much more carefully
how he would deal with faction if and when he encountered
it. This he had obviously not done, and it seemed to the group
that he had been much too ready to trust to luck rather than
foresight and skill in dealing with problems of this kind.

Implications

None of the members of the group felt that the worker had
much hope of getting the district councillor to withdraw his
objection to a representative management committee once he
had made it and the leaders of the other faction had started
arguing with him. If the worker did try, as he did in this case,
he would then in effect be supporting the viewpoint of the
one faction against that of the other, and get himself heartily
disliked by the district councillor in the process, as also happened in the case. The members of the group therefore saw the

K

problem as one of influencing the district councillor's attitude *before* he expressed it at the meeting, and they proceeded to discuss it from that angle.

One member of the group suggested that the worker might have succeeded in doing this if he had prefaced his remarks about the need for a representative management committee by praising all the leaders present, including the district councillor, for their public-spiritedness in being willing to work together for the good of the community by getting a literacy class established for the people of the village. Such a prefatory remark, he thought, would have shamed the district councillor into a willingness to co-operate. The other members of the group, however, thought that the district councillor was much too faction-minded to be put off by any consideration of that kind.

Another member then suggested that had the worker already been aware that faction existed, he might have openly suggested that the leaders might find it difficult to agree to sit on the same managing committee, while stressing that this was essential and that unless they could agree there would be no class. This member thought that the district councillor would then have withdrawn his objection since he wanted the class. Other members, however, thought that what the district councillor wanted was a class which he would run and for which he would get the credit, and that this was the only basis on which he would be prepared to co-operate.

The members of the group then discussed whether the worker could have usefully done anything when the district councillor called on him at his office at the very beginning of the case. They thought that the worker could quite reasonably have been expected to ask the councillor some questions about the number of potential learners, and who was available to teach. At the same time he could have mentioned the need for a representative committee, and had he done so he would almost certainly have discovered the district councillor's objection to it. He could then have tried to get him to change his attitude, and he would have had a better chance of doing so they thought, in the privacy of his office than at the subsequent meeting in the village at which both factions were present. If he had succeeded, his job at the subsequent meeting would have been much easier. If he had failed, he would at any rate have been aware of the kind of difficulty he would be up against, and in the light of this knowledge he might well have decided that under the circumstances it would be useless to go on.

Having reached this conclusion, the members of the group were unhappy with it, for it seemed to them that all that stopped the people having a literacy class, which they really wanted, was the worker's demand that they should also have a representative management committee, to which some of them were very strongly opposed. This led some members of the group to question whether the worker was right to impose this condition as the price of giving his help. (At this point the member who had contributed the case said that it was not he who imposed this condition, but the government for which he worked.) Even if it could be assumed that the worker could succeed in getting the leaders of both factions to serve on the same committee, this would not solve the problem of getting them to work harmoniously together in the management of the class. The only real answer, these members of the group thought, would have been for the worker to have seized on the suggestion one of the elders had made in the case—that there should be *two* classes, one for each faction—and to have added the further suggestion that there should be *two* management committees, one for each class.

This led to much further discussion: some members of the group now feeling that they had at last found a satisfactory solution to the problem, while others felt that on no account should a community development worker appear to sanction and legitimize faction by agreeing to work with two (project) committees each representative of different factions within the same village. However, all members did agree although some of them reluctantly, that this approach seemed to offer the best hope of (i) getting literacy work started in that village; (ii) avoiding the intensification of conflict between the two factions; and (iii) enabling the worker to remain on good terms with the leaders of both factions. This seemed to suggest that in the long run more progress might be made in furthering community development by community development workers recognizing and accepting the reality of faction, where it exists, than by attempting to impose on faction-ridden villages a unitary community organization without regard to the facts.

30. NEGRI VILLAGE

After failing to get two strongly opposed village factions to agree to work together on *any* project, the worker decided to support the project wanted by the larger faction. The other faction then causes the project to fail.

THE CASE

Until quite recently I was in charge of community development work in a rural district which included the village of Negri. In this village lived some five hundred people who were divided between two factions. One of these factions was much smaller than the other, but this was compensated for by the fact that its leader was an influential member of the political party then in power in the government of the country.

I had laboured hard for a long time to get these two groups to work together for the good of the village, but without success, and in the end I gave up trying. Then one day the leader of the majority group told me that they had decided to make a road from the village to the town where they went to market, and that they were prepared to do all the work themselves without any help from the minority group if I would get them a government grant and provide some technical help. I arranged to meet the group to discuss their idea with them, and when I had satisfied myself that they really meant what they said, I promised to help them in any way I could. I therefore supported their application for a government grant. In due course this was approved and shortly afterwards the group started work on the road.

Almost at once there was trouble, for the leader of the minority group sent in a petition demanding that the work should stop as the villagers had begun constructing part of the road on land belonging to one of the members of his minority group. When I went to investigate, I found that what he had said was quite true, and that the landowner was objecting. But then I found out that this man had agreed to the plan for the road and accepted a promise of compensation before ever the project had been sanctioned, and that he had only now changed his mind because of the pressure the leader of the minority group had put on him.

I did my best to get him to change his mind again but he would not, since he was afraid of displeasing his leader. This made me really angry. Knowing that this opposition was only for the sake of opposition and that the project really was for the good of the village I encouraged the majority group to go ahead with their project. However, this immediately led to such a great trouble between the two factions, and to so great a threat to the maintenance of peace and order in that village, that I thought it better to stop the work altogether for the time being. That was more than a year ago and the people are still without their road although they need it very badly.

DISCUSSION OF THE CASE

Diagnosis

The members of the group which discussed this case first noted that not only was the road not built, but that the situation at the end of the case was worse than at the beginning. In fact, the only result of what the community development officer had done had been to worsen the existing bad relationship between the two factions and to arouse the resentment of the minority against himself.

The members of the group thought that whatever the worker had done he could not have ensured that the road would certainly be built since faction in that community was evidently so strong. But some of them thought that he might have increased his chances of success if he had acted differently, and all of them felt that he should at any rate have avoided intensifying the conflict between the two factions and worsening his own relationship with one of them.

His main mistake, the members of the group thought, lay in ignoring the leader of the minority faction. They were not sure why he did this: some thinking that it was because he may already have made up his mind that it was useless anyway even to try to get the two factions to agree to work together; and others that once he had satisfied himself that the majority faction was really in earnest in wanting to build the road, he may have thought that the minority faction was not worth worrying about anyway. At this point, one member of the group suggested that the majority faction may even have wanted to keep the project (and the community development officer!) to itself as a means of attacking the status of the other faction and excluding it from participation in community affairs. If this were so, the members of the group thought, the minority leader would have every reason to feel resentful, and this would make him all the more determined to defeat the other faction's project in any way he could.

The worker's second mistake, once he had decided to ignore the minority faction, was to neglect to satisfy himself that the majority faction's planning was adequate to see the project through. This he obviously had not done, for had he done it he would have known about the arrangements with the landowner, and could then have made sure that the transfer of the land was properly completed, or the line of the road altered, before he committed himself to support the project.

His third mistake, the members of the group thought, was once again to assume that he could afford to ignore the minority leader when the trouble had actually occurred and he had tried but failed to get the landowner to change his mind. Throughout the case, in fact, he seemed always greatly to have underestimated the extent of this man's power and influence.

Implications

Although the members of the group had all agreed that the worker's main mistake had been to ignore the leader of the minority faction, they were initially much less clear about just what he should actually have done. They did, however, agree that in all he did he should have been guided by three main aims. These were

(a) to maintain a personal friendly relationship with *both* faction leaders (this, the group thought, was essential if he was to have any hope of influencing them and healing the breach between them);

(*b*) not to commit himself to support either one of the factions against the other (if he allowed this to happen he would immediately lose any influence that he might otherwise have had *as a neutral* with both factions); and

(*c*) to use his influence as a neutral with the members of both factions in order to get them to work together on some project for the benefit of them all.

Had the worker been guided by these aims, the group thought that he would have acted very differently at his first meeting with the leader of the majority faction. He would certainly have expressed his keen interest and his genuine desire to help, but he would also have inquired whether the leader of the minority faction had been consulted, and if so what his reaction had been. If he had not been consulted, as appeared likely from the group's study of the case, the worker would have stressed the importance of getting the minority leader's support, partly because it would increase the project's chances of success which, after all, was what the majority faction wanted, and partly because unless this were done, it might be very difficult to get a government grant.

Since the majority faction seemed really to want the road and also needed a government grant, the members of the group felt that the community development officer would have had a good chance of getting the majority leader to agree, however reluctantly, that the minority leader should be consulted, and he would then have been faced with the problem of choosing the most favourable situation in which this could be done. The group thought that he should have discussed this problem with the leader of the majority faction, partly because his advice would have been well worth having, but mainly because it would get him actively involved in helping the worker with his plans for getting the two factions to work more closely together.

The members of the group noted that there was quite a wide choice of possible situations, and that some were potentially much more favourable than others. They listed the variety of situations as follows:

(a) the worker with the minority leader;

(b) the worker with both leaders;

(c) the worker with both leaders each supported by a few (or many) of his supporters;

(d) as in (c) above, together with any influential members of the community who were not strongly identified with either faction;

(e) the worker at a meeting of the whole village.

In general, the members of the group thought, the worker would have been wise to aim at a small meeting of not more than two or three members of both factions, together with any influential members of the community who were not strongly identified with either faction. Such a meeting, they thought, would give him the best possible chance of success. Because the meeting was small, it would be easier for him to get the members discussing the community's needs, and not necessarily only for a road; how they could best be met; just what difficulties, e.g. factional attitudes among their followers, prevented the leaders from co-operating for the common good; and how in practice these difficulties could best be overcome.

To the extent that the worker could keep discussion firmly focused on the *community* good—and in this he could hope for support from the more community-minded members—the members of the group thought that both faction leaders would feel under considerable pressure to modify their uncooperative attitudes to each other. At the same time neither could resent what the worker was doing since he would be working solely in the community interest and in no way supporting the interest of either faction against that of the other.

Having agreed that this approach offered the best chance of success, but even so no certainty of success, the group went on to discuss what the worker should have done had all his efforts to reconcile the two leaders failed. Here the members of the group could not agree: some maintaining that he must persist with his efforts to reconcile the two leaders, however long this might take; while others thought that he should then feel justified in supporting the majority faction in its attempt to build the road. This second viewpoint they supported on the grounds that the majority faction, having tried but failed to get the support of the minority faction, would now be demonstrably working, not in its own purely factional interest, but in the interest of the community as a whole: and that it would be quite wrong to allow the minority faction to hold up a project designed to benefit the whole community merely because it persisted in opposition out of factional spite. They did, however, think that the worker would need to be very careful to avoid underestimating the power of the minority faction's leader as the worker had done in the case; and that he should very carefully check each stage of the planning to ensure that the project would succeed in spite of whatever the minority faction might do to try to wreck it.

31. POLITICS AND PEOPLE

Local political party leaders turn the people against a project they had previously wanted to undertake. The worker interviews the leaders to win them over but does not succeed.

THE CASE

We have no separate community development department in my country and it is left to us district administrative officers to do what we can to encourage community projects. I used to manage this quite well on the whole, but I find this particular job much harder now that an electoral system has been introduced and rival political parties have started taking an interest in village affairs. This case is a fairly typical example of the sort of problem I have to cope with nowadays.

Last year I visited a village in my district during the rainy season and found that the people were all very keen to build a road to link their village with the main road some five miles away. I discussed the project with them and promised them some bags of cement for the culverts, and they decided to start work as soon as the rains had finished.

When the rainy season ended and they were due to start work, I received a letter from their headman to say that the people were now refusing to do anything because the local leaders of two of the newly-formed political parties had been telling the people that they would be fools if they built the road, and that government ought to build it for them out of the taxes they paid.

I decided that I had better go out to the village to see the local party leaders and get them to stop making further trouble. There were three of them in that village, the two trouble-makers and the local representative of the party then in power in the government, and I arranged to see them together at the village headman's house.

I gave them all a good talking to, pointing out that only a few months earlier everyone had been keen enough on building the road; that they needed the road badly; that there was absolutely no chance of government building it for them; and that if they did not build it the only ones to suffer would be themselves. I stressed that the road would benefit everybody, whichever party they belonged to, and ended by saying that I hoped that now they realized this they all had enough public spirit to work together for their own good. Many other villages had already built their own roads and I felt sure that the people of this village would not wish to lag behind the rest.

This speech, however, seemed to have little effect on the attitude of the two leaders who had caused all the trouble. They sat silent and glum, refusing to say anything. Only the local leader of the government party looked pleased as he watched the discomfiture of the others. The village head then said that he thought the leaders would want to consult their followers before they could definitely commit themselves, and on this understanding the meeting came to an end.

A few weeks later I heard from the village head that the two leaders were still turning the people against the project, telling them that the purpose of my visit had been to force the people to build the road, but that I had had to go away without achieving anything since I no longer had any power over them. For all the good I did I might just as well not have gone at all. That road is still not built.

DISCUSSION OF THE CASE

The members of the group thought that the two local political party leaders had probably opposed the project because it was the policy of their parties to discredit the party controlling the government in any way they could, and therefore, *inter alia*, to discredit its community development policy of encouraging and helping village people to help themselves. This they could most easily do by persuading the people, as they had done in this case, that the government was trying to trick them into agreeing to build a road that the government itself ought to build.

The members of the group agreed that this kind of problem was becoming very common in many countries, and that it was difficult to deal with, but they also agreed that in this case the administrative officer had not handled it very well. Thus they thought that he should not have seen the party political leaders by themselves. The very fact that these men had their own strong private motives for influencing the people against the project made it very unlikely that they would respond to any direct appeal he might make in the hope of getting them to change their attitude. What he most needed to do, therefore, and what he also had the best chance of doing, was to weaken their influence with the people, and this seemed to the group to imply that he should have discussed their attitude to the project with the people themselves.

Implications

The members of the group then went on to discuss in greater detail what they thought the worker should have done. Many of them felt that he should have tried to arrive at the village the day before the meeting in order to get at the real facts before attempting to deal with the problem at a more formal meeting the next day. How true, for instance, was what the village head had told him? Had the party leaders actually behaved as the village head had said and if they had, had they succeeded in convincing all the people, or only some of them? And what about the people? Did they no longer care whether the road was built or not, or were they refusing to work because they now believed that the government would eventually build it for them? Once the worker had discovered the answer to these questions, the group thought, he would have a much better idea of what line to take at the meeting.

Everyone agreed with this in theory, but several members thought that it might be quite difficult to carry out in practice. What should the officer actually *do*, they asked, in order to get this information? Go round the village from house to house? If so, how would he decide which people to visit first, and what would be the effect on the people he did not visit? Or would he get the village head to invite the more influential of the village people to meet him? If so, what would be the effect on any other influential people the village head may have omitted to invite? And should he try to meet the individual party leaders in the same way, or would this be undesirable? There was some discussion of each of these questions but opinions differed about what the answers should be; and in the end the group agreed that although the questions were important, and needed asking, so much must always depend on local circumstances that only the worker on the spot was really in a position to answer them. As to the meeting itself, the group thought that the worker should have tried to ensure that *all* the village elders or leaders were present and not merely the leaders of the political parties. Nor should he have lectured them and criticized them for not having started work on the project. Much the best approach, the group thought, would have been for him to have avoided any suggestion of blame or criticism, and to have limited himself to stating facts and asking for further information. Thus he might have reminded the people that they themselves had decided to build the road because they felt they needed it badly; and that government had offered to help by providing the cement. He could then have said that he had heard since that they had changed their minds. Did this mean that they no longer wanted the road? He needed to be sure about this in order to know what to do about the cement which had already been allocated to the project. If they had now decided not to go ahead with the project, the cement would have to be re-allocated to a project in some other village. Was this what they really wanted? They were, of course, entirely free to decide provided only that they were able to make up their minds definitely one way or the other.

The group thought that if the worker had acted in this way, some of the people present—those who most wanted the road— would have become worried at the prospect of not getting it, and that no one would have liked the idea of losing the cement to another village. They thought that some of these people at any rate would then have begun to voice the arguments that the party political leaders had used to turn the people against the project, and that this would have given the worker a chance to refute these arguments by stating more facts without directly blaming or criticizing the party leaders. He could have said, for instance, that the tax money was used for many purposes, one of which was to provide the cement (!) but that none of it was anywhere made available to meet the labour costs of making a feeder road from each small village. These were the facts. What they now had to do was to decide what to do in the light of these facts.

If, having made the facts clear, the worker had then left the issue for the people to decide without trying to influence them one way or the other, the group thought that the people who really wanted the road would have started arguing with the rest in favour of building it, and with a much better chance of succeeding than if he had argued in favour of it himself.

CONCLUSIONS

1. *The worker must at all times both remain neutral and be seen to remain neutral in all arguments and quarrels between community factions.*

(In a community divided by faction the worker has an exceptionally difficult and unenviable task. This is because the factions in such a community are more often keener on hindering and opposing one another than they are on working together for the common good. Thus a faction may oppose a community project for no other reason than that a rival faction has declared in favour of it. This is why it is so hard for a community development worker to succeed at all in such communities, however skilful he may be. He has to go on working patiently in the hope of achieving something, while carefully ensuring that in all he does he avoids making matters worse.

The first essential is that he should remain neutral as between factions in all he does within the community, for as soon as he favours, or appears to favour, one faction more than another, he becomes involved and identified with one faction *against* the others, and thereby intensifies the conflict between them. This will happen if through ignorance or for any other reason he works with one faction only as he did in Case 27, *The Rival Leaders*; or helps one faction to achieve its purpose at the expense of another as he did in Case 30, *Negri Village*, and Case 28, *The Majority Vote*.)

2. *The worker must find out whether factions exist before he starts work in the community.*

(The worker in Case 27, *The Rival Leaders*, was new to the community and did not know that factions existed within it. This led him into making the mistake of assuming that the community was a united one, and that in working through the elected headman and his followers he was working with everyone: and by the time he realized his mistake he was identified with the headman's faction and the damage was done. This suggests that before starting work in any community the worker should always try to find out whether faction is present, and if so for what reasons and between what groups. And to this we can add—if we agree with the conclusions reached by the groups which discussed *The Rival Leaders*, *The Majority Vote*, and *The District Councillor*—that the worker should get as much of this information as possible from sources outside the community and before he goes to work in it. This has two advantages: the one, that the information he gets is likely to be more objective; and the other, that he is thereby freed from the embarrassment of asking questions within the community itself.)

3. *The worker must control his natural eagerness to get something done quickly.*

(The bad effects of trying to get something done quickly in spite of the existence of faction are well illustrated in Case 28, *The Majority Vote* and Case 30, *Negri Village*. In both cases the worker, unable to get the factions to agree on *any* project, lost patience and deliberately decided to support a project favoured by one faction only. In neither case did the project succeed, and in both cases the existing conflict between the factions was intensified. Thus the outcome was nothing but harm, and although this does not mean that a worker is invariably wrong n deciding to work with only one faction, if all his attempts to promote agreement between factions fail, it does mean that he should at least make sure that the project can succeed. He has to realize, for instance, that the project is now a factional, not a community, project, and that it will fail if the faction that wants t lacks the resources to carry it through without the support of other factions, as in the case of *The Majority Vote*; or is unable to prevent the other factions from blocking it, as they were able to do in the case of *Negri Village*.)

4. *The worker must take care to choose the most favourable situations in which to work.*

(Although a worker may sometimes feel bound to support a factional project when all his attempts to bring factions together have failed, yet this is always an admission of his failure to succeed in doing his real job of getting people to work together for the good of their community as a whole. But need he always fail? Study of the cases in this chapter suggests that a great deal depends upon his skill, and one important aspect of this skill lies in choosing the most appropriate situation in which to work.

It will make a great difference, for instance, when a worker is trying to get faction leaders to co-operate, whether he tries to influence them together or apart; with or without some of their followers present; in a small private meeting with or without other community leaders present; or in a large public meeting which is open to everyone. Some of these situations may be much more advantageous than others, and it matters a great deal that the worker should have the skill to choose the situation which gives him the best chance of success.

While no general rule can be laid down which will cover every eventuality in every community, it is worth noting that the groups which considered this question in the context of *The Rival Leaders*, *Negri Village*, and *Politics and People*, all thought that the most favourable situation for dealing with faction would be at a meeting of not more than eight or ten people. Some of these would be the faction leaders, but the others would be influential community leaders who were not so strongly identified with any one faction. Such persons, they thought, would be much more likely than the faction leaders to have the interest of the whole community at heart, and therefore to assist the worker in his attempt to get the faction leaders to agree to support a project that would benefit everyone.)

5. *The worker should avoid making any specific statement about what he thinks should be done or how it should be done.*

(But however favourable or unfavourable the situation in which the worker works may be, a great deal will always depend on *how* he works. We have already noted that he should not side with one faction against another, or identify himself with one faction more than with another, for if he does he will only succeed in pleasing one faction at the cost of antagonizing the other. But we must now go further and conclude that at any meeting at which the leaders of opposing factions are present he should not express any specific opinion about what he thinks should be done, or how it should be done, for this is quite likely to have the same adverse effect. This is well illustrated by Case 29, *The District Councillor*, in which the worker committed himself to the view that a representative village committee must be set up to manage the projected literacy class. One faction leader welcomed this idea, but the other (the district councillor) bitterly resented it. This started an argument between the two leaders and, since the worker had already committed himself in support of one side of the argument, it was not really surprising that he was unable to get them to agree. In fact, all he succeeded in doing was to make things worse.)

SUMMARY OF THE WORKER'S FUNCTIONS WHEN DEALING WITH FACTION

The main (negative) conclusion is that the worker must not take sides, but although this is extremely important, by itself it does not achieve anything. The worker must remain neutral, but he must also *do* something, and if it is dangerous for him even to express an opinion—since one faction may support and another oppose it—what then can he usefully and effectively do?

As a friendly, detached and impartial outsider he can in fact do a great deal. Thus he can

1. make sure that the people understand

    (a) that he is anxious to help them, but that what he can do will depend on how willing they are to work together to help themselves; and

    (b) the kinds of practical help he can in fact provide;

2. by asking questions stimulate the people to think about their community needs and what, if anything, they themselves are able and willing to do to meet them;

3. if the people fail to agree, e.g. because of factional differences about what they might do or how it can best be done, help them to explore these differences by

    (a) helping them to get each viewpoint stated, acknowledged and understood, and by asking questions help to ensure that its merits and demerits are objectively considered and discussed;

    (b) himself contributing to the discussion relevant *facts* of which the people themselves may be unaware;

    (c) suggesting the right of people to disagree until some basis of agreement really acceptable to all is found;

    (d) summarizing the course of the discussion from time to time to indicate on what points (if any) agreement appears to have been reached, and also the areas of disagreement that still remain;

    (e) encouraging people to explore every possible way of resolving their differences to the satisfaction of them all, e.g. as in Case 29, *The District Councillor*, by getting them to consider the idea of having two classes, each with its own management committee; and

    (f) making sure that the people all realize that they themselves will be the only losers if after all they fail to agree. (As was suggested in the commentary on Case 31, *Politics and People*.)

It is worth noting that these are all *positive* functions which the worker can undertake in the community interest, and that none of them is incompatible with the worker maintaining the strictest neutrality between opposing factions.

L

CHAPTER NINE

Asking for Help

So far we have studied only the worker's problems in dealing with the people among whom he works. In this chapter, however, we shall be studying some of the problems he commonly encounters when dealing with other workers. Such workers may be either voluntary or paid: and if they are paid, they may be either colleagues working in his own agency or department, or workers employed by some other agency or department. He has to rely a great deal on voluntary helpers or leaders because there is always so much more to be done than he can ever do himself; and he needs the help of other paid workers whenever he needs to provide some specialist skill or resources that he has not got himself. His problems arise when some worker whose help he needs gives it too little, or too late, or in the wrong form, or not at all.

32. THE DISSATISFIED VOLUNTEERS

The worker fails to convince some disgruntled volunteers that they should go on working without pay.

THE CASE

I am a community development officer and when my Government decided on a literacy campaign I was given the job of organizing adult literacy classes in my district.

I started work in only a few villages, but the idea soon caught on, and when requests for classes started coming in from other villages I was naturally very pleased.

The council of one such village wrote in to say that it had no fewer than seventy illiterates wanting to learn. I went to this village as soon as I could and explained what the council and the learners would have to do.

I said that each learner would have to pay for his own primer, exercise book and pencil, and that it would be up to the council to find suitable volunteers who would be willing to teach without pay. Once these conditions were met then I would be glad to provide blackboards and chalk and show the teachers what to do. I also said that the classes should meet for two hours three times a week for the next six months.

At first all went well. Three suitable young men volunteered to teach and when I had shown them what to do they each took a class for nearly four months. Then I heard that they had suddenly refused to teach any more unless they were paid, and that all attempts to get them to change their minds had failed.

Of course, I went out at once to do what I could. I called the three men together and pleaded with them to go on teaching for the remaining two months. I realized that they must be getting tired, I said, but surely after having already done so much they could agree to finish the job now. However, they were adamant. 'The Government pays you,' they said, 'and we have decided that if it wants the adults of this village taught to read and write then it must pay us too.'

I tried to explain that what they were doing was to provide a community service in their spare time; that that was why it should be done free; and that my situation was quite different from theirs since I was a whole-time worker. All they had been doing, I said, was to help neighbours and friends who would be equally ready to help them.

They said that this was not so and that nobody helped them. For instance, they had to pay fees to the Government if they sent their children to school, and money to the blacksmith if he repaired their tools. Since they had to pay for the services they got, they said, they should be paid for the services they gave.

I argued with them for a long time, but in the end I had to come away without achieving anything. Those men have not done another hour's teaching from that day to this, and what's more, the trouble soon spread to the other villages too. Nowadays, people seem to be interested only in what they can get, and the educated ones are worst of all. What can one do with people like that?

DISCUSSION OF THE CASE

Diagnosis

The members of the group which discussed this case first considered why the teachers gave up after serving satisfactorily for so long. Two possibilities were suggested. One of them was that they may not have wanted to do this work, and that they had only agreed because the village council was able to bring some kind of pressure to bear on them. If this were so, they were never really volunteers at all and would be only too glad of any excuse for giving up. This suggestion, however, did not find favour with most of the members of the group. If there had been pressure, they thought, and if it had been strong enough to make the men work for four months, then it was also likely to have been strong enough to cause them to go on working for the remaining two months.

The second suggestion was that the men may well have been genuine volunteers, but that they had committed themselves without realizing just how much work they would actually have to do; and that they found the work becoming increasingly burdensome as week succeeded week and month succeeded month until they reached the stage of refusing to work any longer. It was also suggested that a major contributory factor may have been that neither the community development officer nor the members of the village council had shown much interest in or appreciation of what the teachers were doing, so that they had come to feel that everyone was taking their work much too much for granted. If this were so, it was not so much the amount of work that the teachers were objecting to—after all, they were still apparently willing to go on working if they were paid—as lack of the recognition which they felt to be their due.

If this were indeed the true explanation, then it is easy to understand why the community development officer failed to get the men to resume work, for all he did in effect was to tell them that he thought they ought to be willing to go on giving their services under the same conditions as before: and he had no really convincing answer when they pointed out that neither he nor their neighbours provided *their* services free, and that all they wanted was to be treated in the same way as everyone else.

Implications

When the members of the group came to consider the implications of their diagnosis, they thought that the trouble might not have occurred at all if only the worker had made sure that the men really were volunteers; that they fully understood just what they would be committing themselves to and for how long; and that they would receive some adequate recognition for the work they would be doing, both while they were doing it and when they had completed it.

The members of the group all felt that the first two points were very important, and they noted that the community development officer would have had ample opportunity to implement them since he had anyway to meet the men before the beginning of the course in order to train them for their work. The third point, however, was discussed at much greater length as the members of the group were not all agreed about just what they thought it should imply.

Several suggestions were made. The first of these was that the community development officer should certainly have done more to encourage the men and show interest in their work by visiting them as often as he could: and that he should also have stressed to the members of the village council how important it was that they too should visit the classes; take an interest in the progress of the learners; and compliment the men on all the good work they were doing.

The second suggestion was that the men should have been told when the classes were started that the village council would arrange a public ceremony at the end of the course when the people who had learned to read and write would be given certificates, and their teachers presented with some mark of public esteem—a badge or a certificate—in recognition of all the good work they had done. This, some members of the group said, was already common practice in the countries from which they had come.

All members of the group agreed that if the community development officer had acted on these two suggestions the trouble that eventually occurred in the case might well not have happened at all, especially if the village was one in which community feeling was still strong. But some members were not satisfied that this particular village was of that kind. They thought that the younger and better-educated people in the village, such as the literacy teachers in the case, were already money-conscious; and that the best way of ensuring the continuity of the classes would be to arrange for an honorarium to be paid.

In their view, the community development officer was quite wrong to prejudge this issue by telling the village council that the men must not be paid. He should have restricted himself to stating a fact, which was that the *Government* would not pay, and to getting the members of the council to consider carefully what they would do in the light of this fact. He could get them to do this, for instance, by asking if they thought they could get volunteers to work unpaid for the whole length of the course, and by stressing how important it was that the men should go on working right to the very end. He could also raise the question of providing them with some recognition, while leaving it to the council to decide just what form this should take. If they thought that an honorarium would be needed, then it would be up to the council to decide how to provide it: either from its own funds, if the council had any; or by asking the learners to make their own small contributions in money or in kind.

At first, some members of the group were shocked by this viewpoint, for the whole idea of community development as they saw it was that people should work without pay for the good of their community. They therefore thought it quite wrong that any community development officer should ever agree to such voluntary workers being paid, and they argued strongly against the viewpoint of the others. This started a long discussion which ended, however, in general agreement on the following points:

1. that the basic principle of community development is that of *community* self-help;

2. that this implies that *everyone*, having agreed to support a project, should contribute to it according to his means;

3. that such contributions may equally well be given in the form of labour, or materials, or money according to what is most needed and what each individual can most usefully provide; and

4. that the adult literacy classes in the case now being studied could legitimately be regarded as a form of community project,

and therefore as a responsibility of the community as a whole.

Having agreed on these four points, the members of the group also agreed that they could see no reason why *either* the village council *or* the learners should not provide the volunteer teachers with an honorarium. Indeed, unless such an honorarium were offered, the members of the group found it hard to see just how the self-help principle was applied. From their study of the case it seemed to them that the three voluntary teachers had been expected to carry the whole burden of the project on their shoulders, and that no one else did anything but take. Thus even if the volunteers had been willing to go on giving, which as it turned out they were not, the members of the group felt that this was after all a very bad example of community development. For it to have justified this name, they thought, the village council or the learners should have at least *offered* an honorarium which the men could have accepted or not as they pleased: and they also noted that if this had been done, it was most unlikely that the trouble would then have occurred at all.

33. THE PRACTICE SCHOOL

The staff of a rural development training centre unwittingly arouse the resentment of the teachers of a local school. They try to put things right but without success.

THE CASE

I am on the staff of a Rural Development Centre. This Centre was established in my country two or three years ago to train school-teachers to assist with rural development programmes and to introduce into the village schools new and better methods of teaching. At that time these schools were offering only a very narrow and formal curriculum that was not of much use to anyone.

Our Centre was established in a village which already had a school, and this was very useful to us as we were able to use it to demonstrate our new methods and ideas and give our trainees practice in applying them. The village school-teachers also benefited since they now had fewer lessons to take, and at first they were very happy.

We, the staff of the Centre, were also very happy when we saw the classes we were teaching according to our new methods making much quicker progress than the classes taught by the teachers of the school. We felt that we were making a real contribution to the progress of our country.

As time went on, however, it became evident that the head master and teachers of the school had begun to dislike the Centre. They no longer co-operated as well as in the past, and they even went about among the villagers pouring lies into their ears.

We were worried about this and after a time our Principal wrote to the Minister informing him about the trouble that had arisen and asking him to request the headmaster to co-operate better. Accordingly, the Ministry sent him a letter, but this seemed to have little or no effect. Then we had a staff meeting to discuss the problem and decided that the best thing to do would be to invite the headmaster and his staff to a meeting at the Centre in the hope of establishing a more co-operative relationship. We therefore sent a letter to the school cordially inviting the staff to visit us and suggesting the day and time for the meeting.

The meeting hour came and we were ready to receive our guests, but no one turned up. However, the school being very near it was quite easy to send someone to find out if they were coming or not. Only the headmaster was there and since we had sent a messenger to find him he felt obliged to come. We then discussed our problems with him for a long time and found him willing to agree on many things. As a result of this meeting the situation then improved for a short time, but soon it was again as bad as it had ever been before. Could we have avoided this problem if we had acted differently, and if so how?

DISCUSSION OF THE CASE

The group which discussed this case agreed that the type of problem it presented was a very common one, and that it occurred between the training centre staffs and field staffs of many agencies other than those concerned with schools.

Diagnosis

The members of the group started by noting that the case specifically stated that the staff of the school were initially quite happy about the establishment of the Centre in their village, and that trouble only began after the Centre had been established for some time. This made them think that it was the way the staff of the Centre behaved towards the staff of the school that caused the trouble, rather than any resentment on the part of the teachers to the establishment of the Centre as such.

At the same time the members of the group fully recognized that it certainly would not be easy for the staff of the Centre to maintain a happy relationship with the teachers. After all, they would be using the school to train their students in the new and better methods which the Centre had been established to introduce, and these would be very different from the out-of-date methods of the teachers whose classes they would be taking. Also, since these new methods were very much more successful than the old ones, the members of the group thought that they may well have had the effect of making the pupils and their parents realize how inadequate their own teachers' methods were. And this in fact was apparently just what happened, for the member of the group who had contributed the case then admitted that the parents of the schoolchildren who did not get the new teaching soon began to criticize their teachers. This, the members of the group thought, was quite enough to explain why the teachers became resentful, and they also thought that any such feeling would be greatly strengthened if the staff of the Centre introduced their innovations without first explaining and demonstrating them to the teachers and inviting their help and support. In fact, the staff of the Centre would need to be most careful in all their dealings with the teachers if they were to avoid arousing their resentment. Since the teachers did become resentful, however, it was clear that the staff of the Centre had not been careful enough.

Because the case provided no specific information about what the staff of the Centre did or did not do in their dealings with the teachers in the school, the members of the group did not feel that they could usefully take their diagnosis of the causes of the trouble any further. They noted, however, that when the trouble did occur, the action of the Principal in writing to the Minister was most unwise. The only effect of this, they felt, was to worsen still further the bad feeling that had already developed between the Centre and the school, and to doom to failure the subsequent efforts at reconciliation by the staff of the Centre.

Implications

The members of the group then considered the implications of their diagnosis. They thought that the key problem facing the staff of the Centre was to find some way of safeguarding or even enhancing the status of the teachers by actively associating them with their work. They thought that this could best be done if the staff of the Centre made a point of treating the teachers as colleagues; consulting them about whatever changes they wanted to introduce; associating them as closely as possible with the planning of each new development; and seeking their help to put it into effect.

The members of the group felt that this would involve regular meetings between the staff of the Centre and the teachers of the school, and they felt that several such meetings should have taken place *before* any demonstration or practice lessons were given. The purpose of these meetings would be:

1. to explain to the teachers why the Centre had been established and why its staff and students will need to use the school;

2. to recognize that this will create problems for the teachers; to encourage them to state whatever difficulties they can foresee; to discuss with them how these can best be minimized or overcome; and to ask for their help in overcoming them;

3. to offer to help the teachers to master the new methods the Centre's staff will use, e.g. by means of a short course designed especially for them;

4. to suggest that both the teachers and their school will gain in status since it will be the first school in the country to develop on the new lines, and as such be likely to attract much interest and many visitors.

The members of the group felt that if these suggestions had been put into effect, the course of events might have been very different. The teachers would have felt that the staff of the Centre really valued their help and was equally ready to help them, and that they would gain in status through the use the Centre would make of their school. Had these first meetings then been followed by regular subsequent meetings to iron out difficulties as they occurred, and to discuss each projected new development, the chances of trouble arising would have been much more remote: and there would have been no need for the Centre either to appeal to the Minister or to call a belated meeting in the hope of putting things right after they had already gone so badly wrong.

34. THE DISAPPOINTED VILLAGERS

The worker tries to get some technical officers to help with a road-building project, but they say that they are too busy to help.

THE CASE

In my country community development is a responsibility of the Social Welfare Department and we, the officers of the Department, have to try to encourage the people in the villages to undertake community projects. However, the people often need more technical help and advice than we can give them, and in such cases we have to call on officers of other departments for help. If for any reason they either cannot or will not provide it, we then find ourselves in a very embarrassing situation.

Quite recently, for example, the people of a village in a rather flat and swampy district decided to build a feeder road to connect with the main road about two miles away. I could see that they would need technical advice, and I therefore told them that I would try to arrange for the appropriate technical officers to come out to the village to advise them.

As soon as I got back to headquarters I invited the officers whose help was needed to a meeting in the village in a few days' time. I invited one from the Public Works Department to advise on how many cubic yards of burnt earth the people would need to prepare for the surfacing of the road; one from the Drainage and Irrigation Department to advise on how the road could best be drained; and one from the Information Department because the people had had no previous experience of working together on a project, and I thought it would be helpful to show them some films about how people had successfully tackled similar projects elsewhere.

On the day fixed for the meeting only the Information Officer came. He said he was willing to help, but without the help of the others the project could not start.

I then arranged a second meeting. To this meeting the other two officers came, but neither was able to promise any help since they said they were both much too busy with work of their own.

The people were naturally disappointed as they were really very keen on having the road. As for me, I wished I had never encouraged them to want to undertake the project in the first place. Perhaps you could have done better?

Diagnosis   DISCUSSION OF THE CASE

The members of the group which discussed this case started on their diagnosis by trying to understand why the technical officers had been so uncooperative. Two possibilities were considered: the one, that they were genuinely too busy; and the other, that they just did not want to help. It was agreed that the first possibility could not be altogether ruled out, but most members of the group thought that if the two officers concerned had been keen enough they would have managed to provide the necessary help somehow: and if not at once, then after some delay. This led the group to consider why the officers may not have been very keen, and several possible explanations were put forward. Thus one member suggested that the technical officers may not have been very eager to take on extra work merely to build up the status of the Social Welfare Department, since it was that department which was likely to get most of the credit for the project if it was satisfactorily completed. Another member suggested that the Public Works Officer at any rate may well have wondered why the Social Welfare Officer had troubled him at all. Surely, he said, provided the length and breadth of the road and the depth of surfacing material required were known, then the amount of burnt earth needed would be the product of a simple sum that almost anyone could do. Yet another member thought that both technical officers may quite justifiably have resented the Social Welfare Officer presuming that he could commit them to attend a village meeting without first consulting them about the date and time.

A long discussion followed, at the end of which the members of the group were feeling distinctly more sympathetic towards the technical officers, and correspondingly more critical of the behaviour of the Social Welfare Officer, than they had been at first. They noted, for instance, that the Social Welfare Officer not only wanted the help of the technical officers, but that they should make themselves available at a time and place that he had decided on. Thus he asked both the technical officers and the Information Officer to attend a village meeting he had arranged: and while the effect of thus assembling the officers of the three other departments at the village might well have raised the Social Welfare Officer's status with the villagers, the members of the group all felt that attendance at this meeting would certainly have wasted a good deal of these three officers' time. Thus not only would each of them have had to sit through a lot of discussion which in no way concerned him while other aspects of the project were being discussed, but they would all have to use up a lot of time going to the meeting and returning from it: and all, so it seemed to the group, for the greater glory of the Social Welfare Officer. The members of the group felt that the officers would resent this, and that the busier they were the more resentful they would be: so that they would be inclined to think of almost any excuse to justify their non-attendance. Indeed, some members of the group wondered what sort of pressure the Social Welfare Officer had been able to bring to bear to get them to attend even the second meeting.

Implications

The members of the group thought that the Social Welfare Officer would greatly have increased his chances of getting the technical officers to co-operate if he had tried to make it as easy and convenient as possible for them to provide the help he needed. If he had tried to do this, they thought, he would certainly not have asked them all to attend the same meeting, or indeed to attend a meeting at all. All he apparently needed from the Public Works Officer, for instance, was information about how deep the covering of burnt earth should be, and this he could have got quite easily by making a personal call at his office or by phone. And although the Drainage and Irrigation Officer would almost certainly have needed to visit the spot, he would have been much more likely to be willing to do this if the

Social Welfare Officer had asked him if he could fit in such a visit when his work next took him near the village: or, if his work was unlikely to take him out in that direction for some time, if he could arrange for one of his assistants to make the visit for him. At least the technical officer could hardly have resented this approach, since the Social Welfare Officer would be clearly recognizing that he already had plenty of his own work to do.

The group also thought that whether the Drainage and Irrigation Officer would then agree to help or not would also partly depend on how the Social Welfare Officer had behaved towards him in the past. If he had previously been treated as he had been treated in this case, they thought, he might still be unwilling to help.

But what if he was willing to help, but genuinely too busy to do so? The result would then still have been the same as it was in the case. The Social Welfare Officer would still have failed to provide the people with the help he had led them to expect, and by disappointing them he would still have weakened their faith in the idea of self-help and in the willingness of government officers to help them. This was a result that the Social Welfare Officer should try to avoid, for once the villagers were disillusioned he would find it very hard to interest them in any other self-help project in the future. The group then went on to discuss what implications this might have for the Social Welfare Officer.

The main implication, the members thought, was that he should try to reach a general understanding with the technical officers whose help he was likely to need about what kinds of help they would be willing to give, and how and when they could most conveniently provide it. Armed with this knowledge, he would know in advance what kinds of help he could normally rely on, and what kinds of help he would find it most difficult to get. He could then avoid leading the people to expect help of the latter kind just when they wanted it, especially if he knew that the technical officer concerned was already very busy on some departmental programme. The group thought that he would do far less harm by being honest than by hopefully making commitments for others which they either could not or would not keep.

35. THE HOMEMAKERS' CLASS

A local authority official sends a woman worker a group of prostitutes for her homemakers' class instead of the young mothers with babies she had been expecting.

THE CASE

Nearly all the women in my country are illiterate, but schools are now being opened for the education of girls, and quite recently a women's section was established in our Rural Development Department. I am in charge of this section.

I have only a very small staff, but we have already started many women's groups. We have also brought quite a lot of women together on short residential courses to teach them how to organize their groups and to teach them the elements of homecraft, child care and hygiene. The women appreciate our efforts very much, and there are many demands for classes that we cannot yet meet.

We have good support from our Ministry, but we also need the support of our male colleagues and of the Local Government Councils of the areas in which we work. This support is not always forthcoming for some of our male colleagues resent the establishment of the women's section, and some of the Local Government Councils are distinctly uncooperative. They dare not defy the central government outright by refusing to allow our workers into their areas, but they certainly do not always give them all the help they deserve. What follows is an extreme case, but it will serve to illustrate what I mean.

Last year our Ministry instructed me to provide a training course in an area where the Local Government Council had rather surprisingly asked for a course since it had always before been opposed to the education of women. We had no woman worker already in the area, so I wrote to our local rural development officer (male) asking him to contact the officials of the Council, tell them about the course, and get them to select twelve intelligent young mothers who would like to attend it. I also particularly asked him to make sure that the mothers brought their babies with them. In due course he replied that the arrangements had been made, and a date was fixed for the course to start.

I decided to take this course myself, but when I arrived and met the course members I found that they were all prostitutes from the market. You can imagine my feelings! However, I was not angry with the prostitutes for it was not their fault, so I told them that there had been a mistake and that they had better go back to the man who had sent them and tell him so.

The women went off laughing and soon the local government official who had sent them came to see me. He was very angry. He said that even if they were prostitutes and had no babies they were all potential mothers, and that anyway I could teach them sewing or cooking instead of child care. I said that I was certainly not going to waste my time and government money by teaching women like that, and that I had made it perfectly clear in my letter that the course was intended for young mothers with babies. (Later on, however, the rural development officer to whom I had written confessed to me privately that he had not read my letter properly because, he said, it was so long and complicated.) However, when the local government officer saw that I utterly refused to teach the prostitutes and was determined to go back to my headquarters at once, he altered his tone, and begged me not to report adversely to the Ministry about what had occurred. Of course, I could not agree. I reported what had happened when I got back and was instructed that I was to abandon the course.

A few months later I posted a woman worker to this local government area to try again to get some work started, but she failed completely. In fact, she became so depressed that she resigned. Since then we have had to leave this area alone. We know that the women there still long for our help, but what can we do?

Diagnosis   DISCUSSION OF THE CASE

Although the members of the group all sympathized with the worker and felt that her problem was an exceptionally difficult one, they also felt that she had handled it badly with the result that she had made it even worse.

There was some initial discussion about why the Council had ever asked for a women's class since it was known to be strongly opposed to the education of women. Did this imply that the members of the Council had now changed their attitude, or merely that they wanted to make a gesture in order to please the Ministry? Most members of the group thought that the second suggestion was the more likely one, although they did not exclude the possibility that *some* members of the Council may have begun to change their former attitude. But in either case, they felt, the worker should have envisaged the possibility of trouble while doing everything she could to avoid it.

Nor, in view of what was stated in the case, should she have assumed that she could safely rely on the whole-hearted support of the local rural development officer. Indeed, the members of the group thought that her first mistake was to leave him to make all the local arrangements for the course. They felt that in view of what she already knew about him and about the Council she should have found time to make a preliminary visit, meet the Council's officials, explain what was needed, and if possible interview the candidates for the course herself. She would then quickly have found out whether the Council was in earnest or not.

However, she did not do this, and her second mistake, the group felt, was to allow her anger and distress at being faced with a group of prostitutes to get the better of her judgement. All she did from that moment onwards seemed to have been governed by her natural desire to revenge herself on those who had insulted her rather than to educate and influence them to modify their attitude and give her their support.

Implications

In the course of their diagnosis, the members of the group had already agreed that the worker should desirably have personally supervised the arrangements for the course, but they now recognized that this might not have been possible in view of her other commitments. If this were so, they thought that she should at least have stated her requirements as clearly and briefly as possible in the letter she wrote to the rural development officer, whereas in fact she appeared to have written such a long and complicated one in her anxiety to make everything clear that he found it too much trouble to read.

All the members of the group had already agreed in their diagnosis that what she actually did when faced with the group of prostitutes was wrong, but now they found that they were by no means agreed on what she ought to have done. There were two opinions: the one, that she should have accepted the class of prostitutes and taught them sewing or cooking instead of homecraft and child care; and the other, that she was right in refusing to teach them, but should have

M

behaved quite differently when she met the responsible local government official.

Those who held the first opinion argued that if she had accepted the prostitutes all the subsequent trouble would have been avoided, and then later on she might have got the kind of course she really wanted. Most members of the group, however, disagreed. If she had accepted the prostitutes, they said, she would have brought on herself and on her section the ridicule of everyone who had hoped to see her efforts fail, and she would have seriously prejudiced the future progress of the work of her section. Her mistake, they said, was in the *way* she refused them.

How then did she go wrong? First, they said, in sending the prostitutes back to say that she refused to teach them, for they thought it would have been better if she had gone herself. Secondly, and this they thought was her key mistake, in rejecting outright the local government official's plea that she should refrain from sending in an adverse report. They recognized that she did this because she felt that she and her section had been gravely insulted, but thought nevertheless that if only she had had her main purpose clear, e.g. to start up women's work in the area of this local government authority, she would have acted quite differently. She would have said that she did not want to submit an adverse report, but a complimentary one, but that if the course did not take place she would have to explain why. She could then have suggested that perhaps it was still not too late for the course to take place if a few really suitable women could be found. If she had done this, they felt, she might well have got her class.

36. THE HORSE DISEASE

An administrative officer fails to get help from an animal husbandry officer when a disease breaks out among horses belonging to farmers living in an outlying village.

THE CASE

I am a government administrative officer, and when I encountered this difficulty I was in charge of community development work in a

district. I was very fortunate compared with officers of other departments in this district since I had a better house than most of them,
and I alone had a house telephone and a jeep for personal use. The
other officers frequently asked me for the loan of the jeep, but of
course it was provided for my own use. I was responsible for it and
was not supposed to lend it to anyone.

Then one day it so happened that some farmers came to the
district headquarters from an outlying village to tell me that disease
had broken out among their horses. They had been to the animal
husbandry officer, but he had not paid any attention to them, and
that was why they had then come to me. I promised these farmers
that I would arrange for the animal husbandry officer to go out at
once to check the disease from spreading any further.

I immediately wrote officially to the animal husbandry officer
requesting him to visit the area of the outbreak and check the spread
of the disease. I then went on tour for several days, and when I
returned I was told that he had been sending his subordinate to my
office asking for the jeep to take him to the area of the outbreak.
This he had no right to do, so I flatly refused and straight away sent
him another official letter asking him to proceed to the area immediately. He then promised to go, but the next day the same group of
farmers came again to say that most of their horses had now died
and that there was now nothing more to be done. They were very
upset. I feel that I have lost their confidence and I blame the
animal husbandry officer for it.

DISCUSSION OF THE CASE
Diagnosis

The members of the group which discussed this case started
by listing some of the possible reasons why the animal husbandry officer had not attended to the villagers in the first
place. Several reasons were suggested. Thus it was possible that
the villagers had not actually seen the animal husbandry
officer, and that it was one of his subordinates who had sent
them away; or they may not have stated their problem clearly
enough; or the animal husbandry officer may have been
genuinely too busy at the time to give them all the attention
they thought they deserved; or, of course, he may really have
been as lazy and unhelpful as the villagers inferred. The members of the group thought that the first thing the worker should
have done would have been to question the villagers very closely

in order to establish just whom they saw and what had been said at the animal husbandry office: and not, as he seemed to have done, taken what the villagers told him at its face value.

Whatever the cause of the trouble may have been, the members of the group all felt that the way the worker then behaved was most inappropriate. Thus he should not have sent an official letter 'requesting' the animal husbandry officer to do something which he had already told the villagers he could not or would not do. They thought that the animal husbandry officer would strongly resent receiving a letter of this kind from an officer of another department, and that his natural reaction would be to reject it, or if he thought this unwise, then to find some excuse for not doing anything. This would explain his request for the loan of the jeep which he would have known the worker was unlikely to lend. All the same, the worker's flat refusal to lend it and his second letter demanding immediate action would have made the animal husbandry officer even more resentful. The members of the group felt that the worker had behaved throughout as though he had the right to tell the animal husbandry officer what to do, and that this was a very bad way of getting good co-operation. In fact, all the worker had achieved by acting in the way he did was to make matters even worse than before.

Implications

However, the members of the group realized that the fact that the animal husbandry officer or one of his subordinates had already refused help the villagers wanted made it very hard for the worker to take any action without appearing to criticize the animal husbandry officer and take sides with the villagers against him. In fact, they could think of no way in which he could have tackled this problem so as to be *sure* of success, but they did agree on several points which would have given him a better chance. They thought, for instance, that it would have helped a great deal if the worker had previously established a friendly and co-operative relationship with the animal husbandry officer, e.g. by occasionally lending him the jeep, for the animal husbandry officer would be much more likely to listen to him now if he had already helped that officer on some occasion in the past.

They also thought that he should have handled the actual case quite differently. Having questioned the villagers to find out exactly what had happened, he should not have promised them that he would send the animal husbandry officer out to them at once. This committed him to do something he had no power to do and would make his task much more difficult if it came to the knowledge of the animal husbandry officer. The most he should have said was that he would see the animal husbandry officer to find out if anything could be done, and that he would let them know as soon as he could.

The members of the group also thought that the worker should have gone to see the animal husbandry officer instead of writing to him. He should then have raised the subject informally after having carefully thought out beforehand how he could best do so without giving offence. His best hope, they thought, would be to assume that the animal husbandry officer would be genuinely willing to help if he could, but that there was probably some good reason why he could not do all the villagers wanted immediately. Thus his general line of approach in their view should be

(a) to inform the animal husbandry officer that the villagers were apparently badly in need of his help;

(b) to say that he recognized that the animal husbandry officer was doubtless very busy, but that he hoped very much that he could somehow find time to help them, since they were in great trouble; and

(c) to ask if there was any way in which he himself could help, e.g. by lending the jeep to enable the animal husbandry officer to get to the village with the least inconvenience to himself.

37. THE 3-F CAMPAIGN

The Health Department asks the Community Development Department to initiate a 3-F (*Food for Family Fitness*) campaign in a certain village. The Heads of both the Health and Agricultural Departments promise that their local district officers will help, but in fact they do not help.

THE CASE

I am a District Community Development Officer, and the case I am about to describe occurred in my district last year when the Head of my department was asked by the Head of the Health Department to initiate a 3-F campaign in a village where the people were suffering from malnutrition. He agreed to do this on the understanding that the Head of the Health Department, and of the Agricultural Department, would instruct their local officers to do everything they could to help. Since the village was located in my district, I was made responsible for planning the campaign.

The first thing I did was to contact the local health and agricultural officers. They told me that they had heard from their respective departmental heads about the project and that they were quite willing to help.

I had already done some work in that particular village, and therefore knew the leaders and the members of the various village groups. This helped me to get local committees quickly established for publicity, education, and action, and I was soon ready to start the campaign.

However, when these committees asked the local officers of the Health and Agricultural Departments to their meetings, they did not come. All they did was to complain that the times fixed for these meetings were inconvenient to them. I then got the times of the committee meetings changed to suit their convenience, but they still did not come. Then I got my Head of Department to report their conduct to their departmental Heads, but even this had no effect. In fact, I soon discovered that these officers had deliberately started their own projects in neighbouring villages purely in order to have an excuse for not helping me in mine. I also heard that they had been telling their friends that they had no intention of helping me since they did not see why they should work on another department's project for which that department would get all the credit.

This made me work with redoubled energy, and in the end I succeeded without their help. But I really needed their help and they ought to have given it. After all, the Health Department suggested the project in the first place.

Diagnosis

The members of the group which discussed this case thought it typical of many similar cases which, they said, cropped up quite frequently in their own countries: and they suggested three main reasons to explain the conduct of the health and agricultural officers. The first of these reasons was that they were unwilling to exert themselves for a project the credit for which, if it was successful, was more likely to accrue to the Community Development Department than to their own. (This was the reason actually given in the case.) The second reason was that the community development officer had pro-bably done too much of the planning himself with the result that some of the detailed arrangements he had made, such as fixing the times of committee meetings, may have been actually inconvenient to the health and agricultural officers who were expected to attend them. The third reason suggested was that these officers may have felt that the people might assume that they were in some way inferior in status to the community development officer, since he would seem to be acting as officer-in-charge and they as his assistants.

A contributory reason, members of the group thought, was that neither the Head of the Health Department nor the Head of the Agricultural Department felt responsible for seeing that their local officers really exerted themselves to help. In fact, as soon as the Head of the Community Development Department had agreed to sponsor the project, they appeared to have taken no further interest in it.

Implications

When the members of the group went on to discuss implica-tions, some felt that the community development officer's best chance of obtaining co-operation was to bring pressure to bear on the health and agricultural officers so that they would *have* to help. Thus they suggested that he should have found out from the beginning just what instructions they had received from the heads of their departments, and if they had not been specifically ordered to help he should have reported this to his head of department. His head of department could then have asked the heads of the health and agricultural departments to issue more specific instructions which would have obliged their local representatives to co-operate. They also thought that the community development officer should then make it as easy as possible for them to co-operate by inviting them to share in the planning.

The other members of the group, however, did not think that this would solve any of the community development officer's difficulties. They pointed out that the heads of the health and agricultural departments would not like being told what orders they should give, and might well refuse to give them: and that even if they did give them, this would not make the health and agricultural officers *feel* any more co-operative. Indeed, it would probably have quite the opposite effect. The crux of the problem, they felt, was to get these officers to change their attitude to the community development officer and to the project.

This started a long discussion about how this could be done. Thus it was suggested that the problem would not have arisen if the community development officer had invited the health officer to take charge of the project since his department had suggested it in the first place, while promising to help him in every way he could. This would have ensured the health officer's co-operation if he had agreed, as the members of the group thought he would have done, since the main credit for the campaign would then have gone to him.

While everyone thought that this would probably have solved the difficulty with the health officer, some thought that there were other difficulties it would not solve. The community development officer himself might not like handing over control of the project. Indeed, his head of department might not allow it, and even if he did the problem of getting the co-operation of the agricultural officer would still remain unsolved.

This led to further discussion about how these two difficulties could be overcome, and the group gradually came round to the opinion that what was most needed was some clear under-standing and agreement *between* departments about the exact role that each should play in inter-departmental projects of this kind. The group thought that there was always likely to be bad feeling if, when an officer of a technical department suggested a project as in this case, it was handed over to the community development department to carry out with the technical departmental officer still expected to be willing to give any help that the community development officer might require. As this was primarily a health project and initially proposed as such by the health department, the group thought that the health officer should have been put in charge of it. Similarly, had a primarily agricultural project been proposed by the agricultural department, they felt that the agricultural officer should have been put in charge of it. Had this principle been generally accepted and consistently applied, they thought, much of the friction between the community development officer and the officers of the technical departments would have disappeared. The community development department would then have been recognized as a department which was as ready to help technical departments on *their* projects as it was to ask help from technical departments on projects of its own. Also, each department would have been getting its fair share of status and credit for the work it had done, and this after all, is the only basis on which really effective co-operation between depart-ments can be expected to develop.

CONCLUSIONS

In all the cases included in this chapter, the worker made the mistake of assuming that because he was doing community work this gave him the *right* to expect help from other people and that these other people therefore had a duty, not only to give it, but to provide it as and when the worker wanted it.

Whatever we may think of this assumption in theory, it is clear that it was a very misleading one in the context of each of these cases, for in no case was it borne out by the facts. These were that none of the people whose help the workers needed were really keen to give it, and still less to agree without question or argument to all the workers wanted them to do. Nor could the workers force them, although in at least two instances, in Case 33, *The Practice School* and in Case 37, *The 3-F Campaign*, the workers tried. To succeed, therefore, the workers needed to win their willing co-operation and this was what none of them had realistically tried to do.

Several general conclusions are suggested by the cases. These can be briefly stated as follows:

1. *The worker should always consult an officer of another department and get his consent before committing him to provide help on a group or community project.*

(In both Case 34, *The Disappointed Villagers* and Case 36, *The Horse Disease*, the worker seems to have assumed in effect that he was free to decide what an officer of another department should do, and without regard to the fact that that officer might already be very busy with his own departmental commitments. In both cases the worker seems to have aroused the resentment of the officers concerned, and in neither case did they provide the help he wanted.)

2. *When asking for help, the worker should not demand it as of right even if he has, or thinks he has, the power to do so.*

(The effect of doing this, except in an acknowledged superior–inferior relationship, is nearly always to arouse resentment and a non-cooperative attitude in the person whose help the worker needs. In effect, the worker is then claiming priority for himself and his purposes, and presuming to deny the other person the right to decide freely for himself. This implies that the worker considers that the status and purposes of the other person are inferior to his own. This implication seems to have been resented both by the schoolteachers in Case 33, *The Practice School*, and by the animal husbandry officer in Case 36, *The Horse Disease*).

3. *The worker should ask officers of other departments for help only when he really needs it, and then at the convenience of the officer whose help he seeks rather than his own.*

(If the worker feels he has a *right* to be helped, he may

sometimes be tempted to ask for help when he does not really need it, or for more help than he really needs, or for the help to be given at a time or place that suits his convenience rather than that of the person he expects to provide it. The extent of the worker's demands on the technical officers in Case 34, *The Disappointed Villagers* is a case in point, for if the worker had merely asked the public works officer what depth of burnt earth would be needed on the road he would have troubled him hardly at all. Instead he asked him to attend a village meeting to discuss the project and at a time that was already fixed. By going to such a meeting the public works officer would have had to waste a good deal of his time and this he was quite unwilling to do.)

4. *When the worker knows before he starts work on a project that he will need to call on other people for help, he should either invite them to share in the planning or alternatively submit his plans to them for comment.*

(In Case 33, *The Practice School*, the Principal of the Rural Development Centre knew in advance that he was going to need the co-operation of the school-teachers, and in Case 37, *The 3-F Campaign*, the community development officer knew that he would need a great deal of help from the health and agricultural officers. Yet in each case the worker planned the project and took decisions affecting the people whose help he was going to need without inviting them to share in his planning, or even to comment on the decisions he wanted them to put into effect.)

5. *The worker must aim to ensure that all those who help him on a project get their full share of credit for whatever help they give, even if this means getting less credit for himself.*

(In all the cases included in this chapter, the people who withheld co-operation had several reasons for withholding it: and in most of the cases one of these reasons was that they felt that someone else was getting—or would get—most of the credit for the work they were being asked to do. The fact that the health and agricultural officers in Case 37, *The 3-F Campaign*, started with this attitude suggests that they had already had experience of this when they had helped on projects in the past: and it is worth noting that although the literacy class teachers in Case 32, *The Dissatisfied Volunteers*, and the school-teachers in Case 33, *The Practice School*, did not *start* with this attitude, the fact that they felt that they got no proper recognition for the work they did soon produced exactly the same attitude in them also.)

6. *The worker should keep his main purpose in mind, and therefore his natural resentment under control, when the help he asks for is not forthcoming.*

(When the worker is denied help by someone from whom he feels it should be forthcoming, he is liable to feel resentful. He then needs to remind himself of his main purpose as a worker, so that the resentment he feels will not lead him to act in a way that will make matters even worse. Thus if he wanted help but has not got it, then presumably he still wants it and he should therefore ask himself just why he has so far failed to get it, and just what he can now most realistically do in order to succeed where he has so far failed. Had the woman worker in Case 35, *The Homemakers' Class*, asked herself this question, she would have behaved very differently and might have significantly increased her chances of success. Similarly, had the worker in Case 32, *The Dissatisfied Volunteers*, asked himself the same question, he might then have seen the situation of the literacy class teachers as *they* saw it. He might then have tried to find some way of satisfying them instead of trying to impose on them his own idea of how voluntary workers should behave.

The conclusions listed above are all statements of points that workers can profitably bear in mind when they find themselves actually in need of help during the course of their work and by observing them they can avoid many causes of failure. But however well they may behave at the time that they need help, whether they then get it or not will also very largely depend on how they have behaved in the past towards those whose help they need now—on how friendly they have been, for instance, and on how ready to give help when others have needed it. If a worker has already earned for himself a reputation as a friendly, helpful and unassuming officer, he is then far more likely to get help and co-operation from others.)

CHAPTER TEN

Summary of Conclusions

ALTHOUGH the community development worker may need to acquire some technical skills—for example, in developing countries he may need to know something about agriculture or methods of road-making or building construction—his basic and primary skill is in working with people. This is a particularly difficult and complex skill to learn. No one community or community group is quite the same as any other, and therefore the worker cannot ever be sure that what he has succeeded in doing in one community he can do with equal success in another: and one lesson that all the cases teach is that in this field of work it is the people, not the worker or his agency, who are in control. If the worker attempts to impose his demands he will fail. He has to take the people as he finds them—whether they are good or bad, co-operative or uncooperative, keen or apathetic—and use what skill he has in the hope of educating and influencing them for the 'better'. He has to work with them at their own pace and on their terms. He needs time as well as skill, and we have to recognize that however hard and skilfully he works he will sometimes fail. In community work it is the people, not the worker, who are the final authority.

While this is true, it is also true that sensitivity to the feelings, attitudes, and relationships of the people, realism in deciding what best to do, and skill in doing it, will greatly increase a worker's chances of success. What this sensitivity and skill imply in practice has been discussed in some detail in the commentaries to the cases, and now it only remains to summarize the general conclusions to which they lead.

1. Even when people have already chosen a project, and need only a little encouragement and help to go ahead, the worker

still needs to check that the project will meet a real and permanent need. (*See especially Case 1.*)

2. The worker needs to be able to convince people that he really is keen to help them even while he is trying to dissuade them from undertaking a project which he thinks is badly chosen and therefore likely to fail. (*See especially Case 3.*)

3. The worker must not assume, because the people seek his advice, that all he has to do is to give it, for they will not take it unless they think it good. His real job, therefore, is to help them find a solution acceptable to themselves. (*See especially Case 2.*)

4. The worker must be careful to draw the people's attention to factors which they would otherwise overlook, but which they need to take into account when deciding what to do. (*See especially Case 4.*)

5. The worker should not assume, if the people readily agree to a project he suggests, that they therefore want it and will genuinely do their best to carry it through to a successful conclusion. (*See especially Cases 6, 7 and 8.*)

6. The worker should make sure that the project has and can keep the support of everyone whose help will be needed. (*See especially Cases 5 and 7.*)

7. While the worker is right to highlight the advantages of any innovation he may suggest, he should not try to 'sell' it to the people by stressing only these advantages. Rather he should try to establish for the innovation *a favourable balance of advantage* in the light of all the facts, both favourable and unfavourable, from the people's point of view. (*See especially Cases 9, 10, 11, 12, 13, and 15.*)

8. The worker should avoid arousing resentment by attempting to decide for people something they feel they have the right to decide for themselves. (*See especially Case 14.*)

9. When seeking to establish a group in relation to *his* purposes the worker must realize that he will fail unless he can ensure that it will adequately meet, and go on meeting, some actual need or purpose of the people he hopes will join. (*See especially Cases 16 and 18.*)

10. When forming a group the worker needs to be able to

anticipate any major difficulties the group is likely to have to face, and to help the group to think out how they can be avoided or overcome. (*See especially Cases 17 and 19.*)

11. When helping a group to plan a programme or choose a project, the worker must try to ensure that every viewpoint and suggestion is adequately considered. (*See especially Case 20.*)

12. The worker must at all times try to remain acceptable to all the members of any group with which he works. (*See especially Cases 20 and 21.*)

13. The worker must avoid appearing to criticize the way the members of a group conduct their meetings by relating any suggestions for improvement to the good qualities of the group's members rather than to any of their specific shortcomings. (*See especially Case 21.*)

14. The worker needs to give as much or more attention to leaders who do not sympathize with his aims as to those who do. (*See especially Cases 23 and 24.*)

15. The worker must try to ensure that the changes he promotes, and the way he promotes them, do not adversely affect the status of the people's traditional leaders. (*See especially Cases 23 and 25.*)

16. The worker should not appear to favour any one leader at the expense of any rival leaders. (*See especially Case 26.*)

17. The worker must at all times both remain neutral and be seen to remain neutral in all arguments and quarrels between community factions. (*See especially Cases 27, 28 and 30.*)

18. The worker must find out what factions exist in a community before he starts active work in it. (*See especially Cases 27, 28 and 29.*)

19. Wherever faction exists the worker must curb his natural eagerness to get things moving quickly. (*See especially Cases 28 and 30.*)

20. The worker must be careful to choose the most favourable situations in which to work. (*See especially Cases 27, 30 and 31.*)

21. Where faction exists the worker should always avoid giving his own opinion about what should be done or how it should be done. (*See especially Case 29.*)

22. The worker should always consult an officer of another department and get his consent before committing him to provide help on a group or community project. (*See especially Cases 34 and 36.*)

23. When asking for help, the worker should not demand it as of right even if he has, or thinks he has, the power to do so. (*See especially Cases 33 and 36.*)

24. The worker should ask officers of other departments for help only when he really needs it, and then at the convenience of the officer whose help he seeks rather than his own. (*See especially Case 34.*)

25. When the worker knows before he starts work on a project that he will need to call on other officers for help, he should either invite them to share in the planning or alternatively submit his plans to them for comment. (*See especially Cases 33 and 37.*)

26. The worker must aim to ensure that all those who help him on a project get their full share of credit for whatever help they give, even if this means getting less credit for himself. (*See especially Cases 32, 33 and 37.*)

27. The worker should keep his main purpose in mind, and therefore his natural resentment under control, when the help he asks for is not forthcoming. (*See especially Cases 32 and 35.*)

The cases from which these conclusions have been drawn have been contributed by workers from many countries, and accepted as typical of their own problems by workers from an even wider range of countries. It would seem, therefore, that many of the problems of community and extension workers in every country are basically the same. If that is so, and if the conclusions set out above are soundly based on the cases, this suggests that these conclusions are likely to be relevant for community workers everywhere.